The iPod Playlist Book

A musical starter kit for your portable player

Clifford Colby, editor

Peachpit
Press

THE IPOD PLAYLIST BOOK

Peachpit Press
1249 Eighth Street
Berkeley, CA 94710
510/524-2178
510/524-2221 (fax)
Find us on the World Wide Web at: www.peachpit.com
To report errors, please send a note to errata@peachpit.com

Peachpit Press is a division of Pearson Education
Copyright © 2005 by Peachpit
Editors: Robert Benjamin, Clifford Colby, Karen Reichstein
Production Editor: Lupe Edgar
Copyeditor: Elissa Rabellino
Compositor: Interactive Composition Corporation
Cover and Interior design: Charlene Charles Will

ISBN 0-321-30469-1

9 8 7 6 5 4 3 2 1

Printed and bound in the United States of America

Contents

Contents

V

Introduction

WE LOVE LISTS.

Here's a great collection of playlists, organized around two broad categories: songs for occasions and situations, and songs from artists and musical styles our list makers especially love.

The lists of songs for occasions and situations can serve as your musical starter kits: Songs to Play at a Cocktail Party, Songs to Play During the Christmas Season, Songs to Play After Getting Dumped.

The songs from artists and musical styles are pretty easy to make out, too: Jonathan Richman songs and Charles Mingus tunes, for example. We tried to not always compile obvious lists, figuring you can walk into your local record store and buy Rolling Stones greatest-hits CDs.

Our first rule guiding the list makers was that they had to want to listen to those songs. A collection of songs, for example, that mention Watergate would be interesting, but most of us couldn't for the rest of our lives hear Billy Joel singing "We Didn't Start the Fire." So we don't have Essential Watergate Songs.

A second rule: The songs had to be available for purchase—you can buy the songs in this book either from a legal online music source, such as the iTunes Music Store, or at your largish local music store.

Originally we'd intended to list tunes alphabetically, and that's what you'll see in some of our lists. In many cases, however, our list makers were adamant that the songs should be heard in a particular order, and so we organized the songs that way.

Every list reflects its maker. At the bottom of each list are the initials of who assembled the list. See "Who Wrote the Book of Lists" for information on the nearly three dozen folks who created this book.

And as with all lists, reasonable folks can have different opinions about songs and artists. That's OK: If you've got a opinion, visit this book's companion Web site at www.peachpit.com/playlistbook and let us hear it.

Even if you agree with everything, still check out the companion site, because it has links to songs in this book that you can purchase on the iTunes Music Store. Enjoy the music!

—The Editors

THE FOLKS WHO CREATED THE PLAYLISTS:

(AP) When he's not playing bass guitar with his band, Andrei Pasternak is perfecting his air guitar chops by the glow of the iTunes interface. "There's so much less equipment needed to play air guitar," Andrei says. "I'm thinking I may make the switch permanently. Now if I can just convince my drummer, Matt, to start playing the air drums."

(AZ) Antonia Zotti is a tango enthusiast who dances at San Francisco Bay Area milongas as often as she can.

(BM) Becky Morgan grew up listening to the Beatles' White Album, going to symphony concerts at Heinz Hall in Pittsburgh, and singing along with Fantastiks records. This accounts for her dangerous habit of immoderately mixing music genres.

(BW) Bob Waugh has always worked at taste-maker radio stations. He is program director at WRNR in Annapolis, Maryland. Before WRNR, he was assistant program director and a DJ at WHFS in Washington, D.C. He worked at WXRK in New York and was a disc jockey at WLIR on Long Island.

(CB) Christopher Breen is editor in chief of Playlistmag.com—a Website devoted to digital music—a contributing editor for *Macworld* magazine, and author of *Secrets of the iPod and iTunes,* 5th edition (Peachpit Press, 2004). He is also a professional musician, performing in the San Francisco Bay Area.

(CC) After four years of college radio, Clifford Colby moved into the more restful job of editor with Peachpit Press.

(CN) Cary Norsworthy is an armchair DJ who maintains a massive vinyl-and-CD collection that spans four decades of reckless shopping habits.

(DM) Dan Mitchell is a music fan and journalist who writes about business, politics, and culture—sometimes all at once. He lives in Minneapolis.

(DS) Dan Strachota has written about music and culture for *SF Weekly, East Bay Express, San Francisco Magazine,* Nerve.com, and *The Wave.* He really likes making lists.

(GF) Grant Faulkner is a writer living in Berkeley, California, who finds most of his happiness in states of melancholy. He also plays the trombone.

(JH) 'Fessa John Hook is a well-known broadcaster in the Southeast specializing in Beach and Shag music. He was *Billboard* magazine's Program Director of the Year in 1983 for a Beach Music/Oldies format. Today, 'Fessa Hook heads the Endless Summer Network on the Internet and satellite (www.beachshag.com). His book on the history of Beach and Shag, *Shagging in the Carolinas,* will be available spring 2005.

(JP) John Poultney is a rakish fellow in the San Francisco area who appreciates a good parking spot and a refreshing beverage now and again. He sings and plays guitar in San Francisco's premiere hulabilly group, the Shut-Ins (www.theshutins.com). He collects vintage music of many varieties and maintains a large collection of tikis, hula dolls, and other Hawaiiana.

(JS) Jacob Strohm teaches 5th grade in a urban elementary school in San Francisco. His students teach him all about hip-hop and call everything he listens to country.

(KK) Kristin Kalning is an avid runner, hiker, spinning instructor, and gym rat. When not exercising or thinking about exercising, she can usually be found gulping ibuprofen and applying ice packs to injured body parts.

(KReichstein) Karen Reichstein's favorite childhood songs were "Uncle Albert/Admiral Halsey" by Paul McCartney and Wings and Harry Nilsson's "Me and My Arrow". These days, her favorite playlist contains a lot of Elliott Smith, Nick Lowe, Ryan Adams, and the Smiths.

(KRyer) Kelly Ryer began performing folk music at the age of six in New England, along with her father and twin sister. After studying voice at Smith College, she performed as a soloist and chorus member with several groups, including the Schola Cantorum in Tokyo; the San Francisco Lyric Chorus; and the Lazy Susans. She is now in her fifth season as a soprano with the Grammy-winning San Francisco Symphony Chorus.

(KW) Music, travel, and nightlife writer Kurt Wolff is the author of *The Rough Guide to Country Music,* an encyclopedic overview of the genre, and *Country: 100 Essential CDs.*

(LK) Joe Sixpack (Lawrence Kay) is creator of the pop-culture Website Slipcue.com, which focuses on Brazilian and Cuban music and country and Americana. A 20-year veteran of the San Francisco Bay Area's freeform radio scene, and country music director for Radio@AOL, Joe never met a weird musical genre he didn't like.

(LL) Liza LePage is a 16-year-old high-school student in Portland, Oregon, who is addicted to coffee, her horse, her camera, and her iPod, not necessarily in that order.

(LM) Lynn Mundell isn't a natural blonde, but she can whistle really, really well with the great divas past and present. When she isn't doing that, she's raising two fine sons and writing for businesses and the occasional publication.

(MB) Marjorie Baer is executive acquisitions and development editor at Peachpit/New Riders. She does her best singing solo, accompanied by car radio or by running water and the clink of dishes. She has performed with Otis Redding, Bonnie Raitt, Richard Thompson, Tammy Wynette, and many others, although entirely unbeknownst to them.

(MF) Michele Flannery spent most of her Wisconsin adolescence locked in her bedroom listening to the Sex Pistols, the Pretenders, and the Clash. This led her on a trail of music director positions at community radio stations WORT in Madison, and KPFA in Berkeley, California, and then on to serve as Senior Music Czarina at Spinner.com. She now lives in San Francisco, happily surrounded by stacks of vinyl, CDs, and 7-inch records.

(MHamilton) Mark Hamilton was music director at Spinner/Radio@AOL from 1999 to 2004. Before that, he was music director at KOIT AM/FM in San Francisco from 1990 to 1999 and did production at KOFY TV20/KBWB in San Francisco from 1985 to 1990.

(MHansen) As a trumpet-playing teenager, Mark Hansen regularly had the used jazz section in his local record store to himself as his pals squabbled over the T-Rex albums in the used rock aisle. He is known to inflict his musical preferences on his staff and patients in California, where he is licensed to commit dentistry.

(MHorn) Matthias Horn plays and studies African and Afro-Cuban hand-percussion rhythms.

(MR) Matthew Rothenberg is executive editor with Ziff Davis Internet in New York. Matthew's musical efforts extend back to his manual-typewriter days; his talents as a songwriter, vocalist, guitarist, and bassist powered the commercial failure of the Amazons, the Ho Hos, Three Guys Called Jesus, and Noise 292.

(PT) Paul Thomason has written articles and program notes for most all of the major opera companies in the United States and is a regular on the intermissions of the Metropolitan Opera international radio broadcasts. He seldom sees a vocal recording he doesn't have to have.

(RB) Robert Benjamin: programmer, patriot. He is program manager for rock formats for Radio@AOL. He spent the '90s as program director of WHFS in Washington, D.C./Baltimore. Before that he served as music director at WXRK in New York and was a D.J. at KOME in San Jose, California.

(RL) Rick LePage believes mono is beautiful, would pick "Smoke on the Water" over "Stairway to Heaven," and is most proud of turning his kids on to Joy Division and opening his mind to country music.

(SC) Scott Cowlin is the director of marketing at Peachpit. He is an avid music lover and monkey admirer. He and his wife gear their vacations around traveling to exotic places such as Kenya and Thailand to spend time with his simian pals.

(SH) Susan Forbes Hansen has just celebrated her 25th anniversary in folk radio, with shows on WHUS, in Storrs, Connecticut ("The Sunday Night Folk Festival"), and WFCR, in Amherst, Massachusetts ("Valley Folk").

(SK) Scott Kelby is editor in chief of *Photoshop User* and *Mac Design* magazines; president of the National Association of Photoshop Professionals; and author of numerous bestselling books, including *Photoshop CS Down and Dirty Tricks* and *The iTunes for Windows Book* (with Kleber Stephenson).

(TB) Rock-hardened capitalist Tom Banigan cut his teeth in the early 1970s singing and playing bass in numerous San Gabriel Valley, California, garage bands before graduating to groups that played on Hollywood's Sunset Strip. After starting college as a music major, he consciously sold out and graduated with degrees in science and business. He is now a vice president of NuSil Technology in Carpinteria, California.

(VG) Victor Gavenda studied music history, organ, and harpsichord in the graduate schools of the University of Texas, Austin, and the University of California, Berkeley. He is choirmaster at St. Clement's Episcopal Church in Berkeley.

Road Trippin'

Ever since the first Model T rolled off the assembly line, Americans have been obsessed with two things: the open road, and the music to listen to for the ride. Nowadays, you can listen to what you want, when and where you want it. Some of the songs on this custom-built list deal with the road theme; others just sound good when you pull into the passing lane.

ROAD TRIPPIN', Red Hot Chili Peppers
GOING MOBILE, the Who
BORN TO RUN, Bruce Springsteen
RADAR LOVE, Golden Earring
AUTOBAHN, Kraftwerk
PETER GUNN THEME, Henry Mancini
ROUTE 66, Nat King Cole, Depeche Mode
HIGHWAY STAR, Deep Purple
BORN TO BE WILD, Steppenwolf
HIGHWAY TO HELL, AC/DC
CARS, Gary Numan
ON THE ROAD AGAIN, Willie Nelson
ROADRUNNER, Bo Diddley
ROADRUNNER, the Modern Lovers
ROADHOUSE BLUES, the Doors
I'VE BEEN EVERYWHERE, Johnny Cash
BREAKOUT, Foo Fighters
KING OF THE ROAD, Roger Miller
HOT ROD LINCOLN, Commander Cody
INTERSTATE 8, Modest Mouse
HIGHWAY 61 REVISITED, Bob Dylan
DA DA DA, Trio
PINK MOON, Nick Drake
ROCKAFELLER SKANK, Fatboy Slim
RUNNING ON EMPTY, Jackson Browne
DRIVE ALL NIGHT, Bruce Springsteen

—RB

Raucosity

Sixty minutes of raucous driving music. Best listened to with the windows rolled down at around 80 miles per hour.

LONDON, the Smiths
TEEN ANGST (WHAT THE WORLD NEEDS NOW), Cracker
CASTANETS, Alejandro Escovedo
YOU SHOOK ME ALL NIGHT LONG, AC/DC
PANIC IN DETROIT, David Bowie
(WHAT'S SO FUNNY 'BOUT) PEACE, LOVE AND UNDERSTANDING?
Elvis Costello and the Attractions
I WANNA DESTROY YOU, Soft Boys
TOWN CALLED MALICE, the Jam
DAMAGED GOODS, Gang of Four
THAT'S WHEN I REACH FOR MY REVOLVER, Mission of Burma
INSTRUMENTAL, Galaxie 500
HOTEL CHELSEA NIGHTS, Ryan Adams
EYE OF FATIMA (PT. 1), Camper Van Beethoven
BABA O'RILEY, the Waco Brothers
PRAISE YOU, Fatboy Slim
I WANNA BE ADORED, the Stone Roses

—RL

Twin Nickels
on the Double X: Drive 55 (!) and Listen to Female Singers

Driving tunes don't have to be testosterone-charged, classic rock. Here's a mix of simmering tunes sung by some of the best female artists ever.

I'M GONNA TEAR YOUR PLAYHOUSE DOWN, Ann Peebles
WADE IN THE WATER, Eva Cassidy
IF LOVE WAS A TRAIN, Michelle Shocked
PERFECT, Fairground Attraction
GUIDED BY WIRE, Neko Case
MORNING GLORY, Chrissie Hynde
ROMEO AND JULIET, Indigo Girls
MISSISSIPPI, June Tabor & the Oyster Band
WAYS TO BE WICKED, Lone Justice
LOVE CHILD, the Supremes
BUILDING A MYSTERY, Sarah McLachlan
DOWNTOWN, Petula Clark
THE EMPEROR'S NEW CLOTHES, Sinead O'Connor
SINNERMAN (FELIX DA HOUSECAT'S HEAVENLY HOUSE MIX), Nina Simone and Felix Da Housecat
BRASS IN POCKET, the Pretenders

—RL

3

Space Truckin':
Songs for Flying to Neptune

Face it—you can't even drive to the grocery store without some tunes.

OUTA SPACE, Billy Preston
ROCKET MAN, Elton John
CALLING OCCUPANTS OF INTERPLANETARY CRAFT,
Shonen Knife (or the Carpenters, you pick)
SPACE ODDITY, David Bowie
SPACE TRUCKIN', Deep Purple
WHITEY ON THE MOON, Gil Scott-Heron
ACROSS THE UNIVERSE, the Beatles
THE MEANING OF LIFE, Eric Idle
SPACEMAN, Harry Nilsson
UNDER THE MILKY WAY, the Church
TELSTAR, the Tornados
PLANET CLAIRE, the B-52's

—DM

Driving Down
the Pacific Coast Highway

It starts below the Oregon border, runs along the central coast of California, and ends above the Mexican line. Don't take it if you want to get somewhere soon.

TWO LANE HIGHWAY, Pure Prairie League
MENDOCINO, Doug Sahm and the Sir Douglas Quintet
MENDOCINO COUNTY LINE, Willie Nelson
SAN FRANCISCO (BE SURE TO WEAR SOME FLOWERS IN YOUR HAIR), Scott McKenzie
SAN FRANCISCO DAYS, Chris Isaak
PACIFICA, Los Straitjackets
ALONE IN SANTA CRUZ, the Ataris
MONTEREY, Eric Burdon and the Animals
ROAD TRIPPIN', Red Hot Chili Peppers
SANTA MONICA, Everclear
L.A. FREEWAY, Jerry Jeff Walker, Guy Clark
WHAT I GOT, Sublime
WHEN THE SWALLOWS COME BACK TO CAPISTRANO, Carmen McRae
PACIFIC COAST HIGHWAY, Burt Bacharach

—LK

That
Lonesome Whistle

The songs are about riding a train, but sometimes (English major alert!) they can be about more than that.

NIGHT TRAIN, James Brown
TAKE THE 'A' TRAIN, Duke Ellington
BLUE TRAIN, John Coltrane
DOWNTOWN TRAIN, Bruce Springsteen
ROCK ISLAND LINE, Leadbelly
WABASH CANNONBALL, Dan Zanes with Bob Weir
MYSTERY TRAIN, Elvis Presley
MIDNIGHT TRAIN TO GEORGIA, Gladys Knight & the Pips
CITY OF NEW ORLEANS, Arlo Guthrie
ORANGE BLOSSOM SPECIAL, Bill Monroe
LAST TRAIN TO CLARKSVILLE, the Monkees
FOLSOM PRISON BLUES, Johnny Cash
DALY CITY TRAIN, Rancid
DRIVER 8, REM
JUMPING SOMEONE ELSE'S TRAIN, the Cure
PEACE TRAIN, 10,000 Maniacs
SHE CAUGHT THE TRAIN, UB40
SLOW TRAIN, Bob Dylan
LOVE IN VAIN, Robert Johnson
THE TRAIN KEPT A ROLLIN', the Yardbirds
TRAIN IN VAIN, the Clash
WAITING FOR A TRAIN, Jimmie Rodgers

—CC

Flyover Country:
Songs for When You're Stuck in Coach

When you're jetting from New York to Los Angeles, do you ever look out the window and wonder just what goes on down there?

LEVELLAND, Robert Earl Keen

NOWHERE ROAD, Steve Earle

NEBRASKA, Bruce Springsteen

FLATNESS, Uncle Tupelo

KEEPER OF THE MOUNTAIN, Flatlanders

COUNTING FEEDCAPS, Greg Brown

THAT'S RIGHT (YOU'RE NOT FROM TEXAS), Lyle Lovett

METHAMPHETAMINE BLUES, Mark Lanegan

OUT HERE IN THE MIDDLE, James McMurtry

OKIE FROM MUSKOGEE, Merle Haggard

CAHOKIAN, Jay Farrar

TALKIN' DUST BOWL BLUES, Woody Guthrie

BECAUSE OF THE WIND, Joe Ely

—DM

Hey,
Where's the Map?

A musical travel planner for your next cross-country road trip.

ANCHORAGE, Michelle Shocked
FRANCES FARMER WILL HAVE HER REVENGE ON SEATTLE, Nirvana
SEATTLE, PIL
OLYMPIA, WA, Rancid
PORTLAND, OREGON, Loretta Lynn and Jack White
DOWN IN OAKLAND, Transplants
DO YOU KNOW THE WAY TO SAN JOSE? Burt Bacharach
LODI, Creedence Clearwater Revival
STREETS OF BAKERSFIELD, Buck Owens
MALIBU, Hole
SAN DIEGO SERENADE, Tom Waits
BARSTOW, Jay Farrar
BY THE TIME I GET TO ARIZONA, Public Enemy
MOTORWAY TO ROSWELL, Pixies
SALT LAKE CITY, the Beach Boys
LUCKY DENVER MINT, Jimmy Eat World
MONTANA, Frank Zappa
OMAHA, Moby Grape
WICHITA LINEMAN, Glen Campbell
KANSAS CITY, Wilbur Harrison
EAST ST. LOUIS TOODLE-OO, Steely Dan
CHICAGO, Frank Sinatra
CLEVELAND ROCKS, Ian Hunter
CUYAHOGA, REM
DETROIT ROCK CITY, Kiss
PANIC IN DETROIT, David Bowie
STREETS OF PHILADELPHIA, Bruce Springsteen
ATLANTIC CITY, Bruce Springsteen
NO SLEEP TILL BROOKLYN, Beastie Boys
DIRTY WATER, the Standells
FIRST WE TAKE MANHATTAN, Leonard Cohen

BALTIMORE, Randy Newman, Nils Lofgren
STREETS OF BALTIMORE, Gram Parsons
CARRY ME BACK TO OLD VIRGINNY, Ray Charles
OH CAROLINA, Shaggy
HOTLANTA, Little Feat
GEORGIA ON MY MIND, Ray Charles
SWEET HOME ALABAMA, Lynyrd Skynyrd
ALABAMY BOUND, Ray Charles
**STUCK INSIDE OF MOBILE WITH THE MEMPHIS
BLUES AGAIN,** Bob Dylan
MISSISSIPPI MUD, Ray Charles
NEW ORLEANS BLUES, Jelly Roll Morton
ALL THE WAY FROM MEMPHIS, Mott the Hoople
AMERICA, Simon and Garfunkel

—RB/BM

New York

New York! Just like I imagined it.

NEW YORK STATE OF MIND, Billy Joel
NEW YORK CITY SERENADE, Bruce Springsteen
AUTUMN IN NEW YORK, Charlie Byrd
NEW YORK MINUTE, Don Henley
NEW YORK, NEW YORK, Frank Sinatra
NEW YORK, NEW YORK, Grandmaster Flash & the Furious Five
NO SLEEP TILL BROOKLYN, Beastie Boys
NEW YORK, Sex Pistols
THIS CITY NEVER SLEEPS, Eurythmics
SPANISH HARLEM, Ben E. King
MONA LISAS AND MAD HATTERS, Elton John
THE BOY FROM NEW YORK CITY, Ad Libs
NEW YORK, NEW YORK, Ryan Adams
FAIRYTALE OF NEW YORK, the Pogues
ANGEL OF HARLEM, U2
JAMAICAN IN NEW YORK, Shinehead
NEW YORK'S MY HOME, Ray Charles
NEW YORK GROOVE, Ace Frehley
NEW YORK CITY, Gil Scott-Heron
ROCKAWAY BEACH, Ramones
JUNGLELAND, Bruce Springsteen

—RB

Los Angeles

It's not really all swimming pools and movie stars.

I LOVE L.A., Randy Newman
LOS ANGELES, X
L.A., Elliott Smith
L.A. WOMAN, the Doors
LOS ANGELES IS BURNING, Bad Religion
WAR WITHIN A BREATH, Rage Against the Machine
SANTA MONICA, Everclear
GOING BACK TO CALI, the Notorious B.I.G.
BOYZ-N-THE HOOD, Eazy-E
BOYZ-N-THE HOOD, Dynamite Hack
COMING INTO LOS ANGELES, Arlo Guthrie
CALIFORNIA DREAMING, the Mamas & the Papas
CALIFORNIA, Phantom Planet
UNDER THE BRIDGE, Red Hot Chili Peppers
VALLEY GIRL, Moon Zappa
WALKING IN L.A., Missing Persons
LOS ANGELES, Frank Black

—RB

Las Vegas

What happens there stays there, but you *can* take the music with you.

VIVA LAS VEGAS, Elvis Presley, Bruce Springsteen, ZZ Top, Dead Kennedys
LET'S GO TO VEGAS, Faith Hill
OOH LAS VEGAS, Gram Parsons
VEGAS, Nico
YOUR LOVE IS LIKE LAS VEGAS, Thrills
QUEEN OF LAS VEGAS, the B-52's
SHOW BIZ KIDS, Steely Dan
HIGH ROLLER, Crystal Method
HIGH ROLLERS, Ice-T
MONEY, Pink Floyd
GIMME SOME MONEY, Spinal Tap (Thamesmen)
MONEY (THAT'S WHAT I WANT), Barrett Strong
LEAVING LAS VEGAS, Sheryl Crow

—RB

Martini Time

The most perfect drink concoction is also the most debated. Shaken? Stirred? Straight up? On the rocks? Olive? Twist? A splash of vermouth? Or should the bottle merely be allowed to sit on the bar? It's been noted that if you ever find yourself on a deserted island looking for company, start making a martini. Someone will soon be along to tell you that you're doing it all wrong.

A WET NIGHT (& A DRY MARTINI), Cynthia Crane and Mike Renzi
DEVIL'S MARTINI, Dynatones
DIRTY MARTINI, Kombo
EVERYBODY THERE WAS DRINKING MARTINIS BUT ME, Hillbilly Hellcats
EYEBALL IN MY MARTINI, the Cramps
IT'S MARTINI TIME, Reverend Horton Heat
MARTINI, Tobin Sprout
MARTINI TIME, the Aqua Velvets
MARTINIS AND BIKINIS, Spies Like Us
ONE WET MARTINI, Jellyroll

—RB

Cocktail Hour

Sure, you can invite the right people, buy the right gin, and get the lights just right. But if you don't have the right music, your party won't get any raves the next day.

TOP HAT, WHITE TIE AND TAILS, Fred Astaire
THE WAY YOU LOOK TONIGHT, Frank Sinatra
NIGHT AND DAY, Ella Fitzgerald
SWINGING ON A STAR, Bing Crosby
I GET A KICK OUT OF YOU, Frank Sinatra
MACK THE KNIFE, Bobby Darin
CRAZY SHE CALLS ME, Nat King Cole
FEVER, Peggy Lee
YOU AND THE NIGHT AND THE MUSIC, Julie London
I LOVE YOU, John Coltrane
WITCHCRAFT, Frank Sinatra
THAT OLD BLACK MAGIC, Louis Prima & Keely Smith
CHEEK TO CHEEK, Ella Fitzgerald and Louis Armstrong
I'VE GOT YOU UNDER MY SKIN, Frank Sinatra
PINK PANTHER THEME, Henry Mancini
IT HAD TO BE YOU, Harry Connick Jr.
(LOVE IS) THE TENDER TRAP, Frank Sinatra
MOON RIVER, Henry Mancini
SOLITUDE, Billie Holiday
MY FAVORITE THINGS, John Coltrane
THEM THERE EYES, Sarah Vaughan
OLD DEVIL MOON, Frank Sinatra
PEEL ME A GRAPE, Diana Krall
STRAIGHTEN UP AND FLY RIGHT, Nat King Cole
BEYOND THE SEA, Bobby Darin
SINCE I MET YOU BABY, Ivory Joe Hunter
YOU'RE GETTING TO BE A HABIT WITH ME, Frank Sinatra
AIN'T THAT A KICK IN THE HEAD, Dean Martin

THE LITTLEST BIRDS, Jolie Holland
STORMY WEATHER, Django Reinhardt
I LEFT MY HEART IN SAN FRANCISCO, Tony Bennett
THEY CAN'T TAKE THAT AWAY FROM ME, Ella Fitzgerald and
Louis Armstrong
THE BEST IS YET TO COME, Tony Bennett
BUONA SERA, Louis Prima
BLACK COFFEE, Ella Fitzgerald

—CC/MHamilton/KRyer

Cole Porter:
The Crème de la Crème

One of the high-water marks of Western civilization is Cole Porter's songs. They sum up, in only a few enchanting bars, what life is all about. It's impossible to ruin one of them, even when you sing it yourself in the shower—but these performances are the essence of true Cole Porter Style, the crème de la crème. A word of warning: Listening to two or more at one sitting is likely to produce the overwhelming urge to have some really good champagne or a perfectly made martini. (That's with gin, *not* chocolate! We're adults here.) Note: Many of these performances are available on a number of collections.

BEGIN THE BEGUINE, Leslie A. Hutchinson
I GET A KICK OUT OF YOU, Ethel Merman
I LOVE YOU, Johnny Desmond
I'M A GIGOLO, Cole Porter (himself!)
IT WAS JUST ONE OF THOSE THINGS, Jo Stafford
IT'S DELOVELY, Mabel Mercer
KATIE WENT TO HAITI, Bobby Short
LOVE FOR SALE, Libby Holman
MISS OTIS REGRETS, Ethel Waters
MY HEART BELONGS TO DADDY, Mary Martin
NIGHT AND DAY, Fred Astaire
WHAT IS THIS THING CALLED LOVE? Lewis Conrad
YOU'D BE SO NICE TO COME HOME TO, Jane Froman

—PT

Tom Waits

Over the past 30 years, Tom Waits has been many things: sensitive singer-songwriter; jazzy bohemian; romantic rock and roller; theatrical composer; noirish storyteller. Throughout, the one thing that's remained constant is his voice—not just his three-packs-a-day purr but also his humorous, loving tone, the one that says all the losers, boozers, and users he chronicles deserve the same chance at happiness.

BETTER OFF WITHOUT A WIFE
BLIND LOVE
BURMA SHAVE
CHRISTMAS CARD FROM A HOOKER IN MINNEAPOLIS
CLAP HANDS
COME ON UP TO THE HOUSE
DIAMONDS ON MY WINDSHIELD
DIRT IN THE GROUND
EGGS AND SAUSAGE (IN A CADILLAC WITH SUSAN MICHELSON)
FRANK'S WILD YEARS
I HOPE THAT I DON'T FALL IN LOVE WITH YOU
INNOCENT WHEN YOU DREAM
JACK AND NEAL/CALIFORNIA HERE I COME
JERSEY GIRL
JOCKEY FULL OF BOURBON
LITTLE RAIN
OL' 55
ROMEO IS BLEEDING
STEP RIGHT UP
SWORDFISHTROMBONES
TEMPTATION
THE HEART OF SATURDAY NIGHT
TIME
WALKING SPANISH
WHAT'S HE BUILDING?
TABLE TOP JOE

—DS

Let's Party!

Let's say you're going out tonight. You're going to party hard, and you want to get pumped up. You need some raucous preparty tunes, some music that's going to get the adrenaline flowing, something with swagger and sex and attitude. Music that goes off before you go out.

ADD IT UP, Violent Femmes
ALL DAY AND ALL OF THE NIGHT, the Kinks
DEBASER, Pixies
FOXY GIRLS IN OAKLAND, Rodger Collins
GET UR FREAK ON, Missy Elliott
GIMME GIMME GOOD LOVIN', Crazy Elephant
HIP HOP HOORAY, Naughty by Nature
IN THE STREET, Big Star
KISS ME ON THE BUS, the Replacements
LAST NIGHT, the Strokes
LET'S GO CRAZY, Prince
LOVE COMES IN SPURTS, Richard Hell and the Voidoids
PARTY HARD, Andrew WK
PARTY OUT OF BOUNDS, B-52's
PARTY PARTY WEEKEND, Joe King Carasco
PUMP IT UP, Elvis Costello
REQUEST LINE, Black Eyed Peas
SHATTERED, the Rolling Stones
TAKE THE SKINHEADS BOWLING, Camper Van Beethoven
TOOTSIE ROLL, 69 Boyz

—DS

Mardi Gras Party

Party ingredients: Hurricanes (the drink, not the other kind), beads, feathers, gumbo, Dixie beer, and a few of these songs.

MARDI GRAS MAMBO, the Hawkettes
CARNIVAL TIME, Al Johnson
DON'T YOU KNOW, YOCKOMO, Huey Piano Smith
GO TO THE MARDI GRAS, Professor Longhair
DO WHATCHA WANNA, ReBirth Brass Band
HANDA WANDA, the Wild Magnolias
BROTHER JOHN/IKO IKO, the Neville Brothers
IKO IKO, Buckwheat Zydeco
BIG CHIEF, Professor Longhair with Earl King
IT'S MARDI GRAS DAY, Gumbo Cajun Band
LUCINDA, the Radiators
MARDI GRAS DAY, Dr. John
MARDI GRAS IN NEW ORLEANS, Dirty Dozen Brass Band
MARDI GRAS ZYDECO, Nathan and the Zydeco Cha Chas
HEY POCKEY WAY, the Neville Brothers
MY INDIAN RED, Dr. John
LET'S GO GET 'EM, Bo Dollis and Monk Boudreaux,
with ReBirth Brass Band
NEW SUIT, Wild Magnolias
SECOND LINE PT. 1, Stop Inc.
YELLOW MOON, the Neville Brothers
TIPITINA, Bo Dollis and the ReBirth Brass Band

—CC/RB

Beyond Danny Boy:
St. Patrick's Day Party

From Dublin to Boston, the Irish have an undeserved reputation for copious drinking and singing. On St. Patrick's Day, you get to do both.

DRUNKEN LULLABIES, Flogging Molly
IRISH LASSES, Ashley MacIsaac
THE IRISH ROVER, the Irish Rovers
THE IRISH ROVER, the Pogues
STREAMS OF WHISKEY, the Pogues
IRISH WHISKEY, Tossers
FUNKY CEILI, Black 47
THE BOYS ARE BACK IN TOWN, Thin Lizzy
JUMP AROUND, House of Pain
THE GANG'S ALL HERE, Dropkick Murphys
FINNEGAN'S WAKE, Dropkick Murphys
KISS ME, I'M #!@*FACED, Dropkick Murphys
SUNDAY BLOODY SUNDAY, U2
COME ON EILEEN, Dexy's Midnight Runners
GIVE IRELAND BACK TO THE IRISH, Paul McCartney
TRADITIONAL IRISH FOLK SONG, Denis Leary
MOLLY MALONE, Sinead O'Connor
TURA LURA LURAL (THAT'S AN IRISH LULLABY), Van Morrison
TOO-RA-LOO-RA-LOO-RAL (THAT'S AN IRISH LULLABY), the Chieftains

—RB

Dinner for Two:
Bossa Nova Style

For many, bossa nova is the music of Brazil (although the country has other wonderful musical styles). If you're preparing a special dinner for two, putting on bossa nova makes you seem hip and cultured. Another bonus point: Unlike Barry White, bossa nova creates a romantic mood without scaring off your date.

AGUAS DE MARCO, Antonio Carlos Jobim and Elis Regina
ALAGOAS, Djavan
BORANDA, Edú Lobo and Tamba Trio
CHEGA DE SAUDADE, Maria Creuza
CORCOVADO, Antonio Carlos Jobim, Astrud Gilberto, João Gilberto, and Stan Getz
DESAFINADO, Antonio Carlos Jobim
DESENCONTRO, Chico Buarque
ILUMINA, Maria Bethania
INSENSATEZ, João Gilberto
ISAURA, Antonio Carlos Jobim
MARIA QUIET, Astrud Gilberto
MANHA DE CARNAVAL, Luiz Bonfa
ONE NOTE SAMBA, Charlie Byrd and Stan Getz
PAPA QUE DIGLADIAR, Jorge Ben
SAMBA DA BENÇÃO, Vinícius de Moraes
SAMBA TRISTE, Baden Powell
SO NICE (SUMMER SAMBA), Marcos Valle
TANTO TEMPO, Bebel Gilberto
THE GIRL FROM IPANEMA, Astrud Gilberto, João Gilberto, and Stan Getz
VALSA DE UMA CIDADE, Os Cariocas
WAVE, João Gilberto

—CC

Piping Hot!

Cooking is a delicate business. Timing is important; getting the right measurements is a must; chopping off your fingers is a no-no. That's why you need background music that won't impede the task at hand. But you also want songs that are fun and lively in order to keep you happily toiling away. If the tunes are food themed as well, that's an added bonus.

BAKE MY PIE, Vinnie & the Stardusters
CANDY, Foxy Brown
CANTALOOP, US3
DELICIOUS, Jim Backus
EAT IT, Weird Al Yankovic
ELEPHANT CANDY, the Fun and Games
FUNKY CHICKEN, Rufus Thomas
GREAT GREEN GOBS, Penn Jillette
HOT NUTS (GET 'EM FROM THE PEANUT MAN), Lil Johnson
HUNGRY SO ANGRY, Medium Medium
I NEED A LITTLE SUGAR IN MY BOWL, Bessie Smith
ICE CREAM MAN, Van Halen
MAMBO ITALIANO, Rosemary Clooney
MILKSHAKE, Kelis
POPCORN, Hot Butter
SUGAR, SUGAR, the Archies
THAT'S AMORE, Dean Martin
TOO DARN HOT, Ella Fitzgerald
YUM YUM (GIMME SOME), the Fatback Band
YUMMY, YUMMY, YUMMY, Ohio Express

—DS

Cookin' Out:
Beats for Beer and Brats

Don't forget the mustard. These songs should make your guests
come back for seconds.

RACING IN THE STREETS, Bruce Springsteen
RAMBLIN' GAMBLIN' MAN, Bob Seger
SOOKIE SOOKIE, Steppenwolf
HAVING A PARTY, Sam Cooke
SURF CITY, Jan and Dean
GREEN ONIONS, Booker T. and the MGs
DOWN ON THE CORNER, Creedence Clearwater Revival
SOCK IT TO ME, BABY! Mitch Ryder & the Detroit Wheels
BACK IN THE U.S.A., Chuck Berry
AIN'T NOTHIN' BUT A HOUSE PARTY, J. Geils Band
STRUTTIN' WITH SOME BARBECUE, Louis Armstrong

—DM

Fourth of July Party

Sometime during the day—maybe after you've got the barbeque going—throw on a slab of American music.

FOURTH OF JULY, X
FOURTH OF JULY, Soundgarden
PINK HOUSES, John Mellencamp
BORN IN THE USA, Bruce Springsteen
AMERICAN MUSIC, Violent Femmes
AMERICAN MUSIC, Blasters
LIVING IN THE USA, Steve Miller
BORN ON THE BAYOU, Creedence Clearwater Revival
WE'RE AN AMERICAN BAND, Grand Funk Railroad
YOUNG AMERICANS, David Bowie
SATURDAY IN THE PARK, Chicago
AMERICAN WOMAN, Guess Who
AMERICAN GIRL, Tom Petty
KIDS IN AMERICA, Kim Wilde
AMERICAN IDIOT, Green Day
BLEED AMERICAN, Jimmy Eat World
BULLET THE BLUE SKY, U2
STAR SPANGLED BANNER, Jimi Hendrix
AMERICA THE BEAUTIFUL, Ray Charles

—RB

Back-Porch Reggae

These songs go great with a bottle of Red Stripe, a back porch on a hot summer's day, and the volume turned up high.

CHILL OUT, Black Uhuru
DREADLOCKS IN MOONLIGHT, Lee Scratch Perry
ISRAELITES, Desmond Dekker
JAILBREAK, Sly and Robbie
LEGALIZE IT, Peter Tosh
MARCUS GARVEY, Burning Spear
MONEY IN MY POCKET, Dennis Brown
96 DEGREES IN THE SHADE, Third World
POLICE AND THIEVES, Junior Murvin
PRESSURE DROP, Toots and the Maytals
PRIVATE I, Dub Syndicate
RAVERS, Steel Pulse
REGGAE MUSIC, Yellowman
ROOTS RADICAL, Jimmy Cliff
THE HARDER THEY COME, Jimmy Cliff
YOU ARE MY EVERYTHING, Gregory Isaacs
ZIMBABWE, Soul Syndicate

—CC/RB

Marley Family

Although Bob was and is the Marley, his wife Rita and son Ziggy made good music too.

GET UP STAND UP, Bob Marley and the Wailers
BUFFALO SOLDIER, Bob Marley and the Wailers
COULD YOU BE LOVED, Bob Marley and the Wailers
IS THIS LOVE, Bob Marley and the Wailers
JAMMING, Bob Marley and the Wailers
ONE LOVE/PEOPLE GET READY, Bob Marley and the Wailers
STIR IT UP, Bob Marley and the Wailers
I SHOT THE SHERIFF, Bob Marley and the Wailers
THREE LITTLE BIRDS, Bob Marley and the Wailers
WAITING IN VAIN, Bob Marley and the Wailers
BROTHERS AND SISTERS, Ziggy Marley and the Melody Makers
NO WOMAN NO CRY, Bob Marley and the Wailers
KEEP ON PUSHING, Rita Marley
LIVELY UP YOURSELF, Bob Marley and the Wailers
TOMORROW PEOPLE, Ziggy Marley and the Melody Makers
EXODUS, Bob Marley and the Wailers

—CC/RB

Tiki Party

To understand tiki music you must understand Tiki, the Polynesian equivalent of Adam, the first man. Early Polynesian people created idols in his likeness, and these morphed into various gods representing war, love, food, and other important things. When the South Pacific craze took over after World War II, the westerners associated tikis with exotic locales such as Hawaii, Tahiti, and the Marquesas Islands. Combining the tiki imagery with island-inspired food, decor, and music resulted in a Polynesian/tiki lifestyle craze that lasted from the 1950s through the 1970s. The music associated with this craze is characterized by jungle drumming, xylophones, chanting, horns, and a generally exotic vibe. It is sometimes called "exotica" music, and sometimes elements of hula, lounge, or voodoo rhythms creep in, although hula music is actually a separate genre. Nonetheless, we've included some examples of hula here along with tiki, exotica, calypso, and voodoo, incorporating both modern and vintage sounds to get your cocktail party jump-started.

BO MAMBO, Yma Sumac
CARAVAN, Martin Denny
TABOO, Arthur Lyman
THE MILLIONAIRE'S HOLIDAY, Combustible Edison
CARNIVAL OF SOULS, Combustible Edison
PRINCESS POO-POO-LY HAS PLENTY PAPAYA, Alfred Apaka
HAWAIIAN COWBOY, Sol K. Hollywaiians Bright
GIRLFRIEND OF THE WHIRLING DERVISH, Martin Denny
COCONUT WATER, Robert Mitchum
GREEN ROSE HULA, Brothers Cazimero
BALI HAI, Peggy Lee
HENE HENE, Israel Kamakawiwo'ole aka Braddah Iz
HONOLULU BABY, Ka'au Crater Boys
TICO TICO, Esquivel
ALOHA HONOLULU, Poi Dog Pondering
SATAN TAKES A HOLIDAY, Jack Malmsten
VOODOO DREAMS, Les Baxter
HAWAIIAN WAR CHANT, Ella Fitzgerald

—JP

Carolina Beach Music

Its roots go back at least 60 years to the Southeast, where white kids heard black music at the beach. The dance those kids did to this Beach Music went by a variety of names (including the Basic, the Fas' Dance, the Bop, and the Dirty Boogie) before finally settling on the Shag. The dance itself is said to resemble a lazy jitterbug, best done to a soul or R & B tune, hopefully on a beach on a warm night. Today, Beach and Shag music are celebrated at two ten-day S.O.S. (Society of Stranders) events in the spring and fall in North Myrtle Beach, South Carolina, at the National Shag Championships, and in more than 100 Association of Carolina Shag (and Bop) Clubs.

SIXTY MINUTE MAN, the Dominoes
MS. GRACE, Tymes
LITTLE RED BOOK, Drifters
LADY SOUL, the Temptations
BRENDA, O. C. Smith
UNDER THE BOARDWALK, the Drifters
39-21-46, the Showmen
COOL ME OUT, Lamont Dozier
NIP SIP, the Clovers
GREEN EYES, the Ravens
CAROLINA GIRLS, Chairmen of the Board
HELLO STRANGER, Barbara Lewis
A QUIET PLACE, Garnett Mimms and the Enchanters
THANK YOU JOHN, Willie Tee
IT STARTED WITH A KISS, Hot Chocolate
MY GIRL, the Temptations
STAY, Maurice Williams and the Zodiacs
WITH THIS RING, the Platters
COOLING OUT, Jerry Butler
I LOVE BEACH MUSIC, the Embers

—JH

Tasty Waves!

Since the early 1960s, Dick Dale has held the title of King of the Surf Guitar. (He still tours relentlessly—go see him.) He's not the only one, however, who 40 years ago shaped the music of the beach, hot rods, and girls.

BUSTIN' SURFBOARDS, the Tornadoes
CALIFORNIA SUN, the Rivieras
CATCH A WAVE, the Beach Boys
HAWAII FIVE-O, the Ventures
LET'S GO TRIPPIN', Dick Dale and His Del-Tones
MISIRLOU, Dick Dale and His Del-Tones
MR. MOTO, the Bel Airs
PAPA-OOM-MOW-MOW, the Rivingtons
PENETRATION, the Pyramids
PIPELINE, the Chantays
RUMBLE, Link Wray
SURF CITY, Jan & Dean
SURFIN' BIRD, the Trashmen
SURFIN' SAFARI, the Beach Boys
SURFIN' U.S.A., the Beach Boys
WALK, DON'T RUN, the Ventures
WIPE OUT, the Surfaris

—MHamilton

Gems
from the Garage

In the 1960s, bands all over the world were trying desperately to be like the Beatles, the Rolling Stones, or both. Some of these bands came pretty close for a song or two before fading off into obscurity, their 7-inch singles gathering dust in the same garages in which they practiced. In the early 1970s, however, guitarist Lenny Kaye resurrected a handful of these songs, compiling the first *Nuggets* collection and thus spawning a bazillion other archival albums. This global hodgepodge of tunes proved that ragged guitar hooks, yelping vocals, and crazed keyboards were the true universal language.

LET IT OUT (LET IT ALL HANG OUT), the Hombres
FARMER JOHN, the Premiers
MAKING TIME, Creation
GLORIA, Them
OSCILLATIONS, Silver Apples
FIRE BRIGADE, the Move
PICTURES OF MATCHSTICK MEN, Status Quo
LA BALSA, Los Gatos
HOW IS THE AIR UP THERE? La De Das
GANGES A GO-GO, Kalyanji & Anandji
LONDON SOCIAL DEGREE, Billy Nichols
OH HOW TO DO NOW, the Monks
BREAK IT ALL, the Shakers
I'M JUST A MOPS, Mops
SANA BIR SEYLER OLMUS, Erkin Koray
SUTEKINA SANDY, Carnabeats
WHY PICK ON ME, the Standells
DOUBLE SHOT (OF MY BABY'S LOVE), Swinging Medallions
PSYCHO, the Sonics

CAN'T SEEM TO MAKE YOU MINE, the Seeds
LITTLE BIT OF SOUL, Music Explosion
PSYCHOTIC REACTION, Count Five
OUT OF OUR TREE, the Wailers
FORD MUSTANG, Serge Gainsbourg
CAN'T EXPLAIN, Love
LE RESPONSABLE, Jacques Dutronc
A MINHA MENINA, Os Mutantes
HARLEY DAVIDSON, Brigitte Bardot
TIME WON'T LET ME, the Outsiders
BEG, BORROW, AND STEAL, the Rare Breed
LIES, Knickerbockers
LITTLE BLACK EGG, the Nightcrawlers

—DS

The Blues

Maybe the weather has changed. Maybe your woman has left you. Maybe you ran out of milk. For whatever reason, you've got the blues.

3 O'CLOCK BLUES, B.B. King
A GOOD MAN IS HARD TO FIND, Bessie Smith
BOOGY CHILLEN, John Lee Hooker
COME ON IN MY KITCHEN, Chris Thomas King
CROSS MY HEART, Sonny Boy Williams
CROSS ROAD BLUES, Robert Johnson
EVIL GAL BLUES, Dinah Washington
HOLD ON TO YOUR MONEY, Howlin' Wolf
I GOT THE BLUES, Otis Rush
I'M A KING BEE, Slim Harpo
JUST KEEP LOVIN' HER, Little Walter
LET YOUR LIGHT SHINE, Keb' Mo'
MANNISH BOY, Muddy Waters
MATCHBOX BLUES, Blind Lemon Jefferson
MYSTERY TRAIN, Junior Wells
PINETOP'S BOOGIE WOOGIE, Pine Top Smith
SHOTGUN BLUES, Lightning Hopkins
SMOKESTACK LIGHTNIN', Howlin' Wolf
ST. LOUIS BLUES, W.C. Handy
STORMY MONDAY BLUES, T-Bone Walker
TEXAS FLOOD, Stevie Ray Vaughan
THE BLUES IS MY BUSINESS, Etta James
THE THRILL IS GONE, B.B. King

—CC

Pow Pow:
'60s French Pop

Historians often suggest that the French have offered little in the way of modern cultural artifacts, save for decent wine and cheese. This theory completely overlooks the 1960s, when the Gauls released some of the best pop music around. While heavily inspired by British artists such as the Rolling Stones and the Kinks, and such American girl groups as the Supremes, these artists added something extra—a frothy sophistication, a casual hedonism—that was prototypically French.

MOI JE JOUE, Brigitte Bardot
BONNIE AND CLYDE, Serge Gainsbourg
TOUS LES GARÇONS ET LES FILLES, Françoise Hardy
LES CACTUS, Jacques Dutronc
LES CORNICHONS, Nino Ferrer
LAISSE TOMBER LES FILLES, France Gall
LES ROIS MAGES, Sheila
JE DIS CE QUE JE PENSE ET JE VIS COMME JE VEUX, Antoine
ROLLER GIRL, Anna Karina
SEXOLOGIE, Daniel Gerard
JANE B., Jane Birkin
7 HEURES DU MATIN, Jacqueline Taïeb
CES BOTTES SONT FAITES POUR MARCHER, Eileen
UN HOMME ET UNE FEMME, Claudine Longet
POW POW, Andre Brasseur
LA POUPÉE QUI FAIT NON, Michel Polnareff
LES FILLES C'EST FAIT, Charlotte Leslie
ROUGE ROUGE, Christine Laume
LE TOURBILLON, Jeanne Moreau
THE CLAPPING SONG, Les Surfs
LA LA LU, Pussy Cat
PSYCHE ROCK, Pierre Henry
ON NOUS CACHE TOUT, ON NOUS DIT RIEN, Jacques Dutronc
TWIST A ST. TROPEZ, Les Chats Sauvages

—DS

Brazil in the '60s

The 1960s were a schizophrenic time for Brazil, and its music reflected that confusion. With a right-wing dictatorship ruling the country, some artists openly protested (see the wild psychedelic works of the Tropicalistas), while others chose to follow a more careful route (playing the traditional styles of bossa nova and samba). Either way, the songs the musicians created stand as some of the most beautiful ever.

ATLANTIDA, Rita Lee
BABY, Gal Costa
BAT MAKUMBA, Os Mutantes
BERIMBAU, Baden Powell and Vinicius de Moraes
CACARA, Maria Bethania
CEREBRO ELETRONICO, Gilberto Gil
DESAFINADO, Antonio Carlos Jobim
LINDONEIA, Nara Leao
MINHA NAMORADA, Carlos Lyra
O BARQUINHO, Roberto Menescal
O NAMORADO DA VIUVA, Jorge Ben
PARQUE INDUSTRIAL, Tom Zé
PEDRO PEDREIRO, Chico Buarque
SO NICE (SUMMER SAMBA), Marcos Valle
SUPERBACANA, Caetano Veloso
TAO LONGE DE MIM, Os Brazoes
THE GIRL FROM IPANEMA, Astrud Gilberto
VELHO AMIGO, Milton Nascimento

—DS

Ska

Before No Doubt—before even the English Beat—there were 1960s ska artists such as the Skatalites and Laurel Aitken. This first wave ruled Jamaican from 1960 until 1966, before the rock steady and reggae styles took precedence. In its initial form, ska was a cross-pollination of American R & B and the traditional Jamaican mento style (similar to calypso), with soulful vocals, punchy horns, and that distinctive shuffling beat. Never has such glorious music come from such a small time and place.

BARTENDER, Laurel Aitken
BONANZA, Carlos Malcolm
BROADWAY JUNGLE, Prince Buster
CARRY GO BRING HOME, Justin Hinds
DANCING MOOD, Delroy Wilson
FAT MAN, Derrick Morgan
FEEL LIKE DANCING, Lee Perry
GHOST TOWN, Roland Alphonso
HUMPTY DUMPTY, Eric Morris
I'M IN THE MOOD FOR SKA, Lord Tanamo
KING OF SKA, Desmond Dekker
MISS JAMAICA, Jimmy Cliff
MY BOY LOLLIPOP, Millie Small
OH! CAROLINA, the Folkes Brothers
RINGO'S THEME, the Skatalites
RUDY, A MESSAGE TO YOU, Dandy Livingstone
SIMMER DOWN, Bob Marley and the Wailers
SOON YOU'LL BE GONE, the Blues Busters
TRAIN TO SKAVILLE, the Ethiopians
WORLD'S FAIR, Ken Boothe, Stranger Cole, and the Skatalites

—DS

Afro-Cuban Rhythms

There's a great story in the connections between African and Cuban music. African rhythms came to Cuba with the slaves, were infused with Spanish guitar and native influences, and went back in the 1950s and '60s to inspire a renaissance in African music. From the Ivory Coast to Benin, from Senegal to the Congo, Cuban music was instantly recognized and embraced, and today it is arguably the main influence underlying popular African music. Modern African artists, in turn, have taken their music back to the Americas, where it continues to transform the interrelated styles we know as salsa, rumba, mambo, Latin jazz, and much more. Here's a sampling.

NTOMAN, Salif Keita (on *Mandali,* by Africando)
SEY, Thione Seck (on *Mandali,* by Africando)
MAMBO YO YO, Ricardo Lemvo
OCHIMINI, Francisco Aguabella
BÉSAME MAMA, Mongo Santamaria (on *Conga Blue,* by Poncho Sanchez)
CO CO MY MY, Poncho Sanchez
CAFÉ CON LECHE, John Santos
VELERO SIN TIMON, John Calloway
BOLIVIANA, Irakere
EL CUARTO DE TULA, Eliades Ochoa (on *Buena Vista Social Club,* by Ry Cooder)
TOUSSAINT L'OVERTURE, Carlos Santana
DESCARGA TOTAL, Maraca

—MHorn

Tango

Tango originated in Argentina more than 150 years ago. The music itself, however, has a worldwide reach and continues to be reinterpreted by each generation's performers, including the present-day French musical group Gotan Project.

AFICHE, Adriana Varela
AV. DE MAYO, Diego Vainer Fantasias Animadas
AZABACHE, Miguel Caló
BOEDO, Julio De Caro
EL CAPITALISMO FORANEO, Gotan Project
EL HIJO TRISTE, Orquesta de Francini-Pontier
LA YUMBA, Osváldo Pugliese
MI NOCHE TRISTE, Carlos Gardel
MONTSERRAT, Orquesta Del Plata
PARA TI MADRE, Francisco Canaro
POBRE FLOR, Alfredo De Angelis
SANTA MARIA (PEPE BRADDOCK MIX), Gotan Project
TODA MI VIDA, Aníbal Troilo
TRISTEZA MARINA, Carlos Di Sarli
VIEJO CIEGO, Astor Piazzolla

—AZ

Downtempo and
Trip-Hop Starter Kit

What is this cool stuff you've heard playing in that funky coffeehouse or European-style café? You never hear these tracks on the corporate-owned and -operated radio station in your town. If you'd like to re-create that laid-back yet funky electronic vibe in your own environment, here's a list of some essential artists and groundbreaking albums in the downtempo/trip-hop genre to start your collection. You might find other tracks on each album that you define as your personal favorites, but there's no denying it: Once you start getting into the downtempo groove, this stuff is really addictive. Sit back and chill.

WAKE UP (MUSHROOM DIVE REMIX), Waldeck

MEISTER PETZ, Peace Orchestra

MARKUS KIENZL DUB, Honey

RIDERS ON THE STORM, Yonderboi

ILLUMINATION, Thievery Corporation

INCIDENT AT GATE 7, Thievery Corporation

BUSENFREUND, Tosca

WHY DOES MY HEART FEEL SO BAD? Moby

SIGNS OF LOVE, Moby

IN THE WAITING LINE, Zero 7

ELEVATE MY MIND, the Stereo MCs

SEE THE LIGHT, Sofa Surfers

REMEMBER, Air

THE SEA, Morcheeba

INERTIA CREEPS, Massive Attack

—CN

Arabic/Eastern
Grooves

When artists fuse modern electronic dance grooves with traditional music, the results are often better—and way more danceable—than the originals. Electronic beats and percussion loops of exotic instruments are mixing it up with music from all cultures and genres, from opera and classical to ethnic rhythms from countries all over the world. Here are some great grooves with a distinctly Arabic/Eastern flair that you can download and play at your next party to create your own Saharan lounge.

BIRD'S EYE VIEW (RHYTHMIC REMIX), Uman
BOSS TABLA, Transglobal Underground
DUB YALIL, Natacha Atlas
JUST YOU AND I, dZihan & Kamien
KESE KESE, dj Cheb i Sabbah
MAFICH ARABI, Banco de Gaia
MUSTT MUSTT, Nusrat Fateh Ali Khan
NECROMANTRA, Marcator
SADAAMBUSH, Muslimgauze
SIROCCO, Christophe Goze
TELEPHONE ARAB, Dissidenten
THE TRAVELLER, Christophe Goze
THE WARM CHILL, TJ Rehmi
YA RAYAH (SONAR REMIX), Dahmane el Harrachi
YALLA, Natacha Atlas

—CN

Shiny, Happy Music:
Songs for Improving Your Mood

At some point the sad songs aren't doing it for you anymore, and you need something to bring you out of the darkness.

THE 59TH STREET BRIDGE SONG (FEELIN' GROOVY), Simon & Garfunkel

GIRLS JUST WANT TO HAVE FUN, Cyndi Lauper

SUGAR SUGAR, the Archies

OH BOY, Buddy Holly

ABC, the Jackson 5

I'M A BELIEVER, the Monkees

LOVE SHACK, the B-52's

SIGNAL IN THE SKY, Apples in Stereo

I'M INTO SOMETHING GOOD, Herman's Hermits

GOODE TYME, the Negro Problem

GOOD VIBRATIONS, the Beach Boys

GOOD DAY SUNSHINE, the Beatles

IT'S A SUNSHINE DAY, the Brady Bunch

WALKING ON SUNSHINE, Katrina and the Waves

I FEEL GOOD, James Brown

—DM

Beauty Is the
Deceiver

Just because a song is sweet with a beautiful melody doesn't mean it has to be down, acoustic, a cappella, a love song, or a sappy ballad. Here's a selection of some beautiful music that spans genres, time, and space.

FOURTH OF JULY, Dave Alvin
STAND BY ME, Ben E. King
LOST CAUSE, Beck
ALISON, Elvis Costello
IF I HAD $1,000,000, Barenaked Ladies
YOU'RE GONNA MISS ME WHEN I'M GONE, Brooks & Dunn
GET OUT OF TOWN, Caetano Veloso
HERE COMES MY BABY, Cat Stevens
1952 VINCENT BLACK LIGHTNING, Richard Thompson
WAITING IN VAIN, Bob Marley
THIS MUST BE THE PLACE (NAIVE MELODY), Talking Heads
OOH LA LA, the Faces
HERE COMES THE FLOOD, Robert Fripp
IF I HAD A ROCKET LAUNCHER, Bruce Cockburn
HALLELUJAH, Rufus Wainwright
REDEMPTION SONG, Joe Strummer
BLACK IS THE COLOR OF MY TRUE LOVE'S HAIR,
Nina Simone & Jaffa
TANK PARK SALUTE, Billy Bragg
A GIRL LIKE YOU, Pete Yorn
WONDERWALL, Ryan Adams
IF THAT'S ALRIGHT, Uncle Tupelo

—RL

Be a Hero

Opera, being a heroic, larger-than-life art form, has always known how best to celebrate a hero—whether it's a Greek god, a mythological or historical figure, or just an ordinary guy caught in an extraordinary situation. So if you're feeling blah and in need of revving up, or you've just pulled off a great coup and want some "YES!!" music blaring, here's your list.

DI QUELLA PIRA, from Act 3 of *Il Trovatore,* by Giuseppe Verdi.
This is the Granddaddy of All Heroic Arias, capped by a stentorian high C at the end, which the tenor (usually) holds as long as he possibly can. The best performance? Get the one sung by Franco Corelli. *The Very Best of Franco Corelli* and *Heroes,* on EMI, both include "Di quella pira." For the complete *Trovatore,* check out the live 1962 Salzburg performance available on two different budget labels (Gala and Opera d'Oro—both stocked by most good classical record stores and available on the Internet). Corelli is joined by a group of singers—and conductor Herbert von Karajan himself!—the likes of which have not been seen in this opera since.

IN ANGER AND FURY I'LL TURN ON THE FOE, from Act 2 of *Julius Caesar,* by George Frideric Handel.
Janet Baker from the complete opera recording on EMI. Julius Caesar, furious (and sung by a mezzo-soprano), from the guy who gave us *Messiah.*

CESSA DI PIÙ RESISTERE, from Act 2 of *The Barber of Seville,* by Gioachino Rossini.
Juan Diego Flórez, from his album *Rossini Arias,* on Decca. Has this aria been sung so superbly since the opera premiered in 1816? Probably not.

DEBOUT, TROYENS, ÉVEILLEZ-VOUS, ALERTE! from Act V of *Les Troyens,* by Hector Berlioz.
Jon Vickers, from the complete recording on Philips. Aeneas and his Trojan army charging off to conquer Italy.

O MUTO ASIL ... CORRIAM! VOLIAM! from Act 5 of *William Tell,* by Gioachino Rossini.
Luciano Pavarotti, from one of his first albums, *Primo Tenore,* on Decca. It'll explain what all the fuss was about.

ESULTATE! from Act 1 of *Otello,* by Giuseppe Verdi.
Mario del Monaco, from the complete opera on Decca. An exultant Otello returns to Cyprus in triumph. For the extremely adventurous: Check out the 1903 recording of the aria by the tenor who created the role, Francesco Tamagno, on the Opal label's *Francesco Tamagno: The Complete Recordings.* Just don't expect stereo sound.

NESSUN DORMA, from Act 3 of *Turandot,* by Giacomo Puccini.
Franco Corelli in *Turandot* is, if possible, even better than he is in *Il Trovatore* (see above). Again, the aria is on *The Very Best of Franco Corelli* and *Heroes* on EMI. The complete opera with Corelli and the spectacular soprano Birgit Nilsson (who matches him note for note) is available on EMI.

VERACHTET MIR DIE MEISTER NICHT, from Act 3 of *Die Meistersinger von Nürnberg,* by Richard Wagner.
Theo Adam, from the complete recording on EMI. The medieval poet-cobbler Hans Sachs reminding all the good burghers of Nuremberg of the glories of Holy German Art. For (historic) performances so good they would even make a Parisian believe in "heil'ge deutsche Kunst," get Rudolf Bockelmann's 1930 aria recording (on the album *Rudolf Bockelmann,* on Preiser Records) or Friedrich Schorr's 1927 recording (on *Friedrich Schorr sings Wagner,* on Preiser Records).

—PT

A Baker's Dozen:
Vocals No One Should Ever Have to Live Without

Compiled by a passionate—not to say compulsive—collector.

EMBRACEABLE YOU, Ella Fitzgerald with Nelson Riddle
GEORGIA ON MY MIND, Willie Nelson
ARE YOU HAVING ANY FUN? Elaine Stritch
ALL THE THINGS YOU ARE, Johnny Desmond
KEEPIN' OUT OF MISCHIEF NOW, Barbra Streisand
ABENDS IN DER TAVERNA, Wilhelm Strienz
CAN THAT BOY FOXTROT, Millicent Martin and Julia McKenzie
BE MY LOVE, Fritz Wunderlich
I WENT TO A MARVELOUS PARTY, Noël Coward
AUTUMN IN NEW YORK, Jo Stafford
I'LL BE SEEING YOU, Frank Sinatra
I ONLY HAVE EYES FOR YOU, Jane Froman
WHEN I AM LAID IN EARTH, Barbara Bonney

—PT

Sunday Morning
Waking Up

It's the weekend. You have nothing to do but lie around the house. Or you have lots to do, but you can't be bothered to do it until later. You feel like lounging, reading the paper, eating a big fat brunch that will make you seriously consider going back to bed. You want a sound track that's mellow and rooted in jazz or blues, with songs that are languorous, sensual, and content. You want to revel in your lazitude.

BEAUTIFUL CAR, M. Ward
DIAMOND IN THE SUN, Sean Hayes
I PREFER THE TWENTIETH CENTURY, Lucksmiths
JENNIFER JUNIPER, Donovan
MARTHA'S MANTRA, Neil Halstead
NEVER LET YOUR DEAL GO DOWN, Etta Baker
NEW SLANG, the Shins
PERFIDIA, Phyllis Dillon
PUNAHELE, Ray Kane
RAGA MULTANI, Ravi Shankar
SALLY GO ROUND THE ROSES, Holly Golightly
SASCHA, Jolie Holland
SOLITUDE, Louis Armstrong and Duke Ellington
SOUKORA, Ali Farka Toure and Ry Cooder
SWEET THING, Van Morrison
THAT'S MY DESIRE, Hadda Brooks
THE CHILD, Alex Gopher
TIDE IS HIGH, the Paragons
TIME AFTER TIME, Chris Montez
WALTZ FOR KOOP, Koop

—DS

Cleaning the House

Cleaning is not an activity that a lot of people get excited about. Therefore, the songs serving as the sound track for cleaning should be upbeat, catchy, and singalongable. It doesn't hurt if the lyrics involve muck or dirt, or help facilitate escapist daydreams.

BONGO BONG, Manu Chao
BORN TO RUN, Bruce Springsteen
BOX ELDER, Pavement
BRA, Cymande
CHECK YOUR BUCKET, Eddie Bo
CLEAN UP WOMAN, Betty Wright
COMMON PEOPLE, Pulp
DIRT OFF YOUR SHOULDER, Jay-Z
FUN FOR ME, Moloko
GOO GOO MUCK, the Cramps
HANGING ON THE TELEPHONE, Blondie
JANE SAYS, Jane's Addiction
LITTLE WILLY, the Sweet
MIRROR IN THE BATHROOM, English Beat
MISTY MOUNTAIN HOP, Led Zeppelin
MR. BLUE SKY, ELO
PUNK ROCK GIRL, Dead Milkmen
SENSES WORKING OVERTIME, XTC
SUBTERRANEAN HOMESICK BLUES, Bob Dylan
WALK ON THE WILD SIDE, Lou Reed

—DS

White Hot Blondes

At one time or another, it seems like everybody's found some solace in a bottle. Of peroxide, that is. Really, who needs hootch when bleach is the chemical of inspiration. And for the record: There's nothing phony about these blondes...

GET THE PARTY STARTED, Pink
DENIS, DENIS, Deborah Harry and Blondie
LADY MARMALADE, Christina Aguilera, with Lil' Kim, Mya and Pink
JOLENE, Dolly Parton
CAN'T STAND LOSING YOU, Sting and the Police
GANGSTA LOVE, Eve with Alicia Keys
RAY OF LIGHT, Madonna
DON'T SPEAK, Gwen Stefani and No Doubt
BABY I CAN'T PLEASE YOU, Sam Phillips
DOLL PARTS, Courtney Love and Hole
DIAMONDS ARE A GIRL'S BEST FRIEND, Marilyn Monroe
THAT'S JUST WHAT YOU ARE, Aimee Mann
LOVE IS A STRANGER, Annie Lennox and the Eurythmics
JOHN, I'M ONLY DANCING, David Bowie

—LM

Hair Cut

It doesn't matter whether it's the corner barbershop or a painfully hip salon—all haircutting establishments play horrible music. You don't need the added torture. Wherever you go, just make sure that your instructions to your cutter now include not snipping the white wires coming out of your ears.

BAD HAIR DAY PUNX, 30 Foot Fall
SISTER GOLDEN HAIR, America
HAIR, Bad Brains
DEVIL'S HAIRCUT, Beck
HAIR OF THE DOG, Bauhaus
ALMOST CUT MY HAIR, Crosby, Stills, Nash & Young
SHE'S ALWAYS IN MY HAIR, D'Angelo
BAD HAIR DAY, MXPX
HAIRSPRAY QUEEN, Nirvana
BLACK IS THE COLOR OF MY TRUE LOVE'S HAIR, Nina Simone
HAIR, Original Broadway Cast Recording
GOOD HAIR (INTERLUDE), OutKast
HAIR, PJ Harvey
LOOKA, NO HAIR, Professor Longhair
HAIR VITAMINS, Jerky Boys
SHE WEARS MY HAIR, Soft Boys
CUT MY HAIR, the Who

—RB

Spin Cycle:
Music for a Spinning Class

A collection of songs to exercise to, from a real-life spinning class. Guaranteed to raise your pulse rate in a responsible manner while you work yourself into a frenzy.

GOT TO GIVE IT UP (PART 1), Marvin Gaye
DON'T STOP 'TIL YOU GET ENOUGH, Michael Jackson
I WOULD DIE 4 U, Prince
BABY I'M A STAR, Prince
TEARS OF A CLOWN, Smokey Robinson
I FEEL LOVE, Donna Summer
WHAT IS HIP? Tower of Power
MR. BIG STUFF, Jean Knight
BILLIE JEAN, Michael Jackson
IT'S YOUR THING, the Isley Brothers
DON'T LEAVE ME THIS WAY, Thelma Houston
THINK, Aretha Franklin
MERCY MERCY ME, Marvin Gaye
DO RIGHT WOMAN—DO RIGHT MAN, Aretha Franklin

—KK

Lace 'em Up:
Music for a 10K

When you're out running, nothing gets you more motivated than listening to a heart-pumping playlist on your iPod. This race-tested list works out to about 50 minutes.

MAGGIE MAY, Rod Stewart
LUST FOR LIFE, Iggy Pop
EVERY LITTLE THING SHE DOES IS MAGIC, the Police
GET BUSY CHILD, the Crystal Method
GOT GLINT, the Chemical Brothers
HONKY TONK WOMAN, the Rolling Stones
MOONAGE DAYDREAM, David Bowie
STAND, Sly and the Family Stone
HIGHER GROUND, Stevie Wonder
LIVE WIRE, Mötley Crüe

—KK

Sports Anthems:
First Inning

Playing at a park, ice rink, stadium, field, yard, or tailgate party near you.

ALIVE, P.O.D.
AWAKE, Godsmack
BREAK STUFF, Limp Bizkit
CRAZY TRAIN, Ozzy Osbourne
FIRESTARTER, Prodigy
GET THE PARTY STARTED, Pink
GET UR FREAK ON, Missy Elliott
I FEEL GOOD, James Brown
JUMP AROUND, House of Pain
MAMA SAID KNOCK YOU OUT, LL Cool J
MACARENA, Los del Rio
NA NA HEY HEY (KISS HIM GOODBYE), Steam
NOOKIE, Limp Bizkit
PUMP UP THE JAM, Technotronic
ROCK YOU LIKE A HURRICANE, Scorpions
SHOUT, Isley Brothers
THAT'S THE WAY (I LIKE IT), KC and the Sunshine Band
THE POWER, Snap
U CAN'T TOUCH THIS, MC Hammer
WELCOME TO THE JUNGLE, Guns N' Roses
Y.M.C.A, Village People
YOU'VE GOT ANOTHER THING COMIN', Judas Priest

—CC/RB

Sports Anthems:
Second Quarter

OK: So there are *a lot* of sporting events.

AND THE CRADLE WILL ROCK, Van Halen
BANG THE DRUM ALL DAY, Todd Rundgren
CUM ON FEEL THE NOIZE, Quiet Riot
FIGHT FOR YOUR RIGHT, Beastie Boys
GETTIN' JIGGY WIT IT, Will Smith
I LIKE IT LIKE THAT, Tito Nieves
LOW RIDER, War
NO SLEEP TILL BROOKLYN, Beastie Boys
PARTY HARD, Andrew W.K.
PUMP IT UP, Elvis Costello
PUSH IT, Salt-N-Pepa
ROCK AND ROLL PART 2, Garry Glitter
ROLLOUT, Ludacris
STOP THE ROCK, Apollo Four Forty
THE HOUSE IS ROCKIN', Stevie Ray Vaughan and Double Trouble
THE ROCKAFELLER SKANK, Fatboy Slim
UNBELIEVABLE, EMF
WALK THIS WAY, Run DMC featuring Aerosmith
WE WILL ROCK YOU, Queen
WILD THING, Tone Loc
WILD THING, X
YOU DROPPED A BOMB ON ME, the Gap Band

—CC/RB

Sports Anthems:
Third Period

Imagine if we had included English football songs.

ALL STAR, Smash Mouth
BAWITDABA, Kid Rock
CELEBRATION, Kool and the Gang
C'MON N' RIDE IT, Quad City DJs
FAT LIP, Sum 41
GET READY FOR THIS, 2 Unlimited
HOT IN HERRE, Nelly
I LOVE ROCK N' ROLL, Joan Jett
LUST FOR LIFE, Iggy Pop
MASTER OF PUPPETS, Metallica
OH, YEAH, Yello
ONE STEP CLOSER, Linkin Park
PLAY THAT FUNKY MUSIC, Wild Cherry
PUMP UP THE VOLUME, M/A/R/R/S
SMOKE ON THE WATER, Deep Purple
SONG 2, Blur
START ME UP, Rolling Stones
THE MIDDLE, Jimmy Eat World
TUBTHUMPING, Chumbawamba
WE'RE NOT GONNA TAKE IT, Twisted Sister
WHO LET THE DOGS OUT, Baha Men
WHOOMP! THERE IT IS, Tag Team

—CC/RB

Chairman of the Board: Songs for the Skatepark

Drop In, Grind, Olley, Power Slide, Carve, Kickflip: Whatever board you are riding, these are the tried-and-true songs to take along.

HEAVEN IS A HALF PIPE, OPM
WELCOME TO PARADISE, Green Day
WELCOME TO THE JUNGLE, Guns N' Roses
MANTHEM, Bouncing Souls
SURFIN' USA, Pennywise
AWAKE, Godsmack
THE KIDS AREN'T ALRIGHT, Offspring
HIGHWAY TO HELL, AC/DC
BULLS ON PARADE, Rage Against the Machine
MOUNTAIN SONG, Jane's Addiction
PEPPER, Butthole Surfers
DOWN WITH THE SICKNESS, Disturbed
ROCK SUPERSTAR, Cypress Hill
FAT LIP, Sum 41
SABOTAGE, Beastie Boys
LAST RESORT, Papa Roach
IT'S TRICKY, Run DMC
PARANOID, Black Sabbath
SKATE TO HELL, Gang Green
SEPARATION OF CHURCH AND SKATE, NOFX

—RB

Dog Park

Canines can hear sounds that we lowly humans cannot. We don't know if dogs are partial to pop music, but this is our best guess at what dogs might listen to if they figured out how to operate the stereo knobs.

RAIN DOGS, Tom Waits
EVERYTIME THE DOGS BARK, John Cale
GOLDEN RETRIEVER, Super Furry Animals
I WANNA BE YOUR DOG, Iggy Pop and the Stooges
DOGS, Caesar
SLOW DOG, Belly
HOUND DOG, Etta James
DOGS, the Who
DOGSONG, the Be Good Tanyas
DOG, Bare Jr.
DIRTY OLD EGG SUCKIN' DOG, Johnny Cash

—MF

Gorillas in the List

It's not that 2004 is the year of the Monkey in the Chinese calendar. It's not that sock monkeys are such curious objects. It's not that the Man in the Yellow Hat probably should be locked up for animal endangerment. It's that monkeys are so diggity-dang cool.

ANOTHER POSTCARD, Barenaked Ladies
APEMAN, the Kinks
BONZO GOES TO BITBURG, Ramones
EVERYBODY'S GOT SOMETHING TO HIDE EXCEPT ME AND MY MONKEY, the Beatles
GORILLA, YOU'RE A DESPERADO, Warren Zevon
I WANNA BE LIKE YOU (THE MONKEY SONG), Los Lobos
IF I HAD A MILLION DOLLARS, Barenaked Ladies
MONKEES THEME, the Monkees
MONKEY, Counting Crows
MONKEY GONE TO HEAVEN, the Pixies
MONKEY IN YOUR SOUL, Steely Dan
MONKEY MAN, Toots and the Maytals
MONKEY MAN, the Rolling Stones
MONKEY ON MY BACK, Aerosmith
RED RED WINE, UB40
SHOCK THE MONKEY, Peter Gabriel
SPACE MONKEY, John Prine
STRAIGHTEN UP AND FLY RIGHT, Nat King Cole
THE LORD IS A MONKEY, Butthole Surfers
THE MONKEY, Dr. John
THE SMARTEST MONKEYS, XTC
TOO MUCH MONKEY BUSINESS, Chuck Berry
TWEETER AND THE MONKEY MAN, Bruce Springsteen

—SC

Cat Box

What is it about cats that inspire folks to write songs about them? Cats are aloof, finicky, and only too aware of the power of their charm. Cats own you, not the other way around. After all, Iggy Pop never would have sung "I Wanna Be Your Cat."

BIG CAT, the Clean
BIG ELECTRIC CAT, Adrian Belew
CAT HOUSE, Takako Mineikowa
HELLO KITTY, Cub
KITTY IN A COMA, James Superstar Kochalka
KITTY, the Presidents of the United States of America
LOVE CATS, the Cure
LOVE KITTENS, the Jazz Butcher
LUCIFER SAM, Pink Floyd
STRAY CAT STRUT, Stray Cats
THREE LITTLE KITTENS, Bob Wills & the Texas Playboys
YEAR OF THE CAT, Al Stewart

—MF

Pop Goes the Movies

Was the Beatles' first movie, *A Hard Day's Night*, really the first music video? The line between movies and music video can get fuzzy. Here's a handful of songs that seem as much sound tracks for their movies as tunes with video support.

A HARD DAY'S NIGHT, the Beatles, *A Hard Day's Night*
BOHEMIAN RHAPSODY, Queen, *Wayne's World*
BRING ME TO LIFE, Evanescence, *Daredevil*
FOOTLOOSE, Kenny Loggins, *Footloose*
HELP! the Beatles, *Help!*
HERO, Chad Kroeger and Josey Scott, *Spider-Man*
I WILL ALWAYS LOVE YOU, Whitney Houston, *The Bodyguard*
I'VE HAD THE TIME OF MY LIFE, Bill Medley and Jennifer Warnes, *Dirty Dancing*
LOSE YOURSELF, Eminem, *8 Mile*
MISIRLOU, Dick Dale and His Del-Tones, *Pulp Fiction*
MY HEART WILL GO ON, Celine Dion, *Titanic*
OH, PRETTY WOMAN, Roy Orbison, *Pretty Woman*
PURPLE RAIN, Prince, *Purple Rain*
STAYIN' ALIVE, the Bee Gees, *Saturday Night Fever*
TAKE MY BREATH AWAY, Berlin, *Top Gun*
YOU'RE THE ONE THAT I WANT, John Travolta and Olivia Newton-John, *Grease*

—MHamilton

Dinner for Two:
More Songs for Pitching Woo

It's not easy to pick music for a romantic dinner. You want songs that set a mood, but you don't want them to be too intrusive, either. These should fit the bill.

BEGIN THE BEGUINE, Artie Shaw
ANGEL EYES, Frank Sinatra
DRUNK ON THE MOON, Tom Waits
AVALON, Roxy Music
TUPELO HONEY, Van Morrison
LOVELY WAY TO SPEND AN EVENING, Johnny Mathis
ALL THE WAY, Tony Bennett
HOW DEEP IS THE OCEAN? Bing Crosby
GOODBYE PORK PIE HAT, Charles Mingus
MOON RIVER, Johnny Mercer
LADY WHAT'S TOMORROW, Elton John

—DM

Beyond Bliss:
An Operatic List

There are moments in opera that are beyond bliss, when time itself stops and everyone is enveloped in a sort of Never-Never Land. Not surprisingly, many of these ecstatic moments occur when two or more people are singing. Perhaps not all the numbers below will provide you with that special moment—but certainly a few of them will.

THE PRESENTATION OF THE ROSE from Act 2 and **ROSENKAVALIER TRIO** from Act 3 of Richard Strauss's *Der Rosenkavalier*
One of the reasons *Der Rosenkavalier* is so special is that it has not one but two time-stopping moments. In Act 2, "The Presentation of the Rose" is a glittery depiction of two people looking at each other and instantly falling in love. In Act 3, the famous "*Rosenkavalier* Trio" sums up all of love—the beginning, the ending, the resignation, the gratitude, the profundity—in three glorious female voices and a 120-piece orchestra. Get the opera (or the highlights) on Decca conducted by Sir Georg Solti. Some people swear by the 1957 EMI recording, conducted by Herbert von Karajan.

THE FINAL DUET from Giordano's *Andrea Chenier*
This is the musical equivalent of pizza with everything on it, including the anchovies. The 1960 Vienna live performance with Renata Tebaldi and Franco Corelli is incandescent (Opera d'Oro).

O SINK' HERNIEDER from Act 2 of Wagner's *Tristan und Isolde*
There is an excellent reason why the love duet from *Tristan* is considered the greatest love duet of all. Kirsten Flagstad and Lauritz Melchoir (Naxos) will let you in on the secret best, since no one has ever equaled them at it. Birgit Nilsson and Wolfgang Windgassen (DG) do it in stereo.

AU FOND DU TEMPLE SAINT from Bizet's *Les Pêcheurs de Perles*
If not for this duet, *The Pearl Fishers* would be unknown, but who could forget the astonishingly beautiful sound of Jussi Björling and Robert Merrill (RCA) singing together?

EBBEN A TE GIORNO D'ORRORE! from Act 2 of Rossini's *Semiramide*
There are two soprano-mezzo duets in *Semiramide*. The Act 1 duet is
great; the Act 2 is beyond sensational. Even people who don't like
opera get bug-eyed when they hear it. Joan Sutherland and Marilyn
Horne sang it all over the world. Their commercial recording is on
Decca, but Hunt has their 1969 live performance, which topped even
their own impossibly high standards.

GIÀ NELLA NOTTE from Act 1 of Verdi's *Otello*
This love duet is one of the few times in opera when a husband and
wife sing a love duet with each other. It's enough to make anyone
believe in the institution of marriage—until you remember what happens at the end of Shakespeare's *Othello*. The recording with Leontyne
Price and Placido Domingo (RCA) is the top pick.

BIMBA DAGLI OCCHI PIENI DI MALIA from Act 1 of Puccini's
Madama Butterfly
U.S. naval lieutenant Pinkerton woos his just-married young Japanese
bride. By far the best version of this Italian opera love duet is in
German, sung by Fritz Wunderlich and Pilar Lorengar (EMI). It'll sizzle
your stereo and melt your heart.

ABER DER RICHTIGE from Act 1 of Richard Strauss's *Arabella*
Two sisters sing the operatic equivalent of George and Ira Gershwin's
"The Man I Love." No one does it better than Lisa Della Casa and Hilde
Gueden (Decca).

—PT

Not Your Typical
Wedding Songs

So you're getting married. Naturally, you have to choose music for the reception. But you don't want to hear the same old Motown soul and '70s funk tunes; you want to set yourself apart, to dig a bit deeper while still offering good dance music. Maybe you even want to show that you have a sense of humor about this whole until-death-do-us-part thing. Maybe you want to express just how amazed you are to be getting married in the first place. Maybe you just want everyone to have fun.

A LITTLE BIT ME, A LITTLE BIT YOU, the Monkees

AT LAST, Etta James

BACHELOR PAD, Fantastic Plastic Machine

BALL AND CHAIN, Social Distortion

CRAZY LOVE, Van Morrison

EVERYONE I'VE EVER SLEPT WITH, Momus

FINDERS KEEPERS, Salt Water Taffy

GROOVE IS IN THE HEART, Dee-Lite

HALLELUJAH, Jeff Buckley

HOLIDAY INNN, Stereo Total

HOW ABOUT THE BOYS? Arling & Cameron

I KNEW THE BRIDE (WHEN SHE USED TO ROCK 'N' ROLL), Nick Lowe

I SEE YOU BABY, Groove Armada

IF YOU WANT TO BE HAPPY, Jimmy Soul

IN SPITE OF OURSELVES, John Prine and Iris DeMent

IS YOU IS OR IS YOU AIN'T MY BABY? Dinah Washington

LET'S GET IT ON, Marvin Gaye

OOH LA LA, Wiseguys

SWEET PEA, Tommy Roe

TENDERNESS, General Public

—DS

Let's Stick Together:
Songs Celebrating Monogamy, Commitment, and Fidelity

Not every relationship has to end with songs for the freshly dumped.

I WALK THE LINE, Johnny Cash
TAKE IT WITH ME, Tom Waits
VALENTINE'S DAY, Steve Earle
NORTHERN SKY, Nick Drake
CONEY ISLAND BABY, Lou Reed
LIKE A ROSE, Lucinda Williams
OH MY LOVE, John Lennon
IN SPITE OF OURSELVES, John Prine
HOTEL YORBA, White Stripes
OH OH I LOVE HER SO, the Ramones
JE T'AIME MON NON PLUS, Serge Gainsbourg
DRIVE ALL NIGHT, Bruce Springsteen
GOD ONLY KNOWS, the Beach Boys
I'M STILL IN LOVE WITH YOU, Al Green
I MELT WITH YOU, Modern English
ANCIENT LONG AGO, Jonathan Richman

—JS

June 11, 2011

Music for Children

We played Mozart for our first child. Our second child, however, wanted to hear these songs (and others like them). We don't know which kid is smarter. The second one is definitely the better dancer.

A HARD DAY'S NIGHT, the Beatles
AL CAPONE, Prince Buster
ALL AROUND THE KITCHEN, Dan Zanes with Loudon Wainwright III
BABY'S IN BLACK, the Beatles
BACK IN MY ARMS AGAIN, the Supremes
BALLOON MAN, Robyn Hitchcock
BROADWAY JUNGLE, Toots & the Maytals
CAUSE I LOVE YOU, Carla & Rufus
CUT ACROSS, SHORTY, Rod Stewart
DO THE DOG, the Specials
(DON'T GO BACK TO) ROCKVILLE, REM
ERIE CANAL, Dan Zanes with Suzanne Vega
GOVERNMENT CENTER, Jonathan Richman
GUYSBOROUGH RAILWAY, Dan Zanes with Donald Saaf
HOUSE PARTY TIME, Dan Zanes
I WANT CANDY, Bow Wow Wow
LAST NIGHT, Mar-Keys
MYSTERY TRAIN, Elvis Presley
ONE STEP BEYOND, Madness
PETER GUNN, Duane Eddy
PUT THE MESSAGE IN THE BOX, World Party
ROCKET 88, Jackie Brenston and His Delta Cats
SO LONG (IT'S BEEN GOOD TO KNOW YUH), Dan Zanes with John Doe
SPARKY'S DREAM, Teenage Fanclub
THE KIDS ARE ALRIGHT, the Who
TIME IS TIGHT, the Clash
TOO EXPERIENCED, the Bodysnatchers

—CC

Music for Texas Dance Halls:
Having a Fling with Western Swing

During the 1930s, Texas natives Bob Wills and Milton Brown invented an upbeat, dance-friendly sound that was part big-band swing and a whole lotta cowboy.

NEW SAN ANTONIO ROSE, Bob Wills and His Texas Playboys
WON'T YOU RIDE IN MY LITTLE RED WAGON, Hank Penny
SHAME ON YOU, Spade Cooley
TEXAS IN MY SOUL, Tex Williams
SOMEBODY'S BEEN USING THAT THING, Milton Brown and His Musical Brownies
ROLY POLY, Bob Wills
WHO'S SORRY NOW, Milton Brown and His Musical Brownies
TEXAS SAND, Tune Wranglers
MY ADOBE HACIENDA, Louise Massey and the Westerners
PIPELINER BLUES, Cliff Bruner's Texas Wanderers
EVERYBODY'S TRUCKIN', The Modern Mountaineers
A SIX PACK TO GO, Hank Thompson
SWEET JENNIE LEE, Hot Club of Cowtown

—KW

Nashville Radio:
Hat Acts of the 1990s

During the 1990s, Garth Brooks was the hottest ticket in country music, though he wasn't the only Nashville star with a penchant for manly hats and burly arrangements.

BETTER MAN, Clint Black
LONG NECK BOTTLES, Garth Brooks
WHERE THE GREEN GRASS GROWS, Tim McGraw
DON'T ROCK THE JUKEBOX, Alan Jackson
SOMEONE TO GIVE MY LOVE TO, Tracy Byrd
STICKS AND STONES, Tracy Lawrence
FRIENDS IN LOW PLACES, Mark Chesnutt
AMARILLO BY MORNING, George Strait
HIGH AND DRY, Marty Brown
HERE'S A QUARTER (CALL SOMEONE WHO CARES), Travis Tritt
BRAND NEW WHISKEY, Brooks & Dunn
WORKING MAN'S PH.D., Aaron Tippin
WATCHA GONNA DO WITH A COWBOY, Chris LeDoux

—KW

Country Sadness

You're driving down the highway late at night. You just broke up with your sweetheart, or you lost your job, and the stars in the sky seem to be tearing up just like you. The only thing that's going to make you happy is a good dose of melancholy, sung with a twang. It's time to snuggle up with some melodies of despair.

BLUE EYES CRYING IN THE RAIN, Willie Nelson
GOODBYE, Steve Earle
LIL WALLET PICTURE, Richard Buckner
DEAR SOMEONE, Gillian Welch
I'M SO LONESOME I COULD CRY, Hank Williams
SPEED OF THE SOUND OF LONELINESS, John Prine
EASY'S GETTIN' HARDER EVERY DAY, Iris DeMent
SHOPPING FOR DRESSES, Merle Haggard
BRASS BUTTONS, Gram Parsons
METAL FIRECRACKER, Lucinda Williams
THE POET GAME, Greg Brown
IF I NEEDED YOU, Townes Van Zandt
LOVE IS REAL, Virginia Dare
GAME OF BROKEN HEARTS, Tarnation
PORCHLIGHT, Neko Case
NEW FAVORITE, Alison Krauss & Union Station
WHISKEY GIRL, Gillian Welch
MAN OF CONSTANT SORROW, the Stanley Brothers

—GF

The Laid-Off Blues

If you've been laid off, you know what a drag it is to find a new job. If you're lucky, you're cruising along with a fat severance package, sleeping in 'til noon and watching daytime talk shows. While you're at it, why not listen to some music?

CAREER OPPORTUNITIES, the Clash
DOT COM BLUES, Jimmy Smith
GOD DAMN JOB, the Replacements
HEAVEN KNOWS I'M MISERABLE NOW, the Smiths
LOST MY JOB, Alex Chilton
OFFICE SPACE FOR RENT, the Planning Commission
SLACK @!#%, Superchunk
TAKE THIS JOB AND SHOVE IT, Johnny Paycheck
UNEMPLOYMENT, Challenger
WHY DO I NEED A JOB? Bare Jr.
YOU'RE FIRED, Bratmobile

—MF

Cryin' in Your Beer:
Songs for Soaking in Cheap Suds and Salty Tears

When you just can't get over the fact that your baby is gone, there's not much left to do but head to the bar and sing along with these tunes at the top of your lungs. Until they throw you out.

HOWEVER MUCH I BOOZE, the Who
PICTURES OF YOU, the Cure
HERE COMES A REGULAR, the Replacements
LOVE WILL TEAR US APART, Joy Division
JUST LIKE A WOMAN, Bob Dylan
SLEEPLESS NIGHTS, the Mekons
SUPERSTAR, the Carpenters
NIGHTSWIMMING, REM
DOWN WHERE THE DRUNKARDS ROLL,
Richard and Linda Thompson
ONLY THE LONELY, Roy Orbison
DID I TELL YOU, Yo La Tengo
OLD SHOES (AND PICTURE POSTCARDS), Tom Waits

—DM

Old Boyfriends

Everyone's Old Boyfriends (or Old Girlfriends) list would be different, of course. Each is a custom song cycle capturing a series of moments that, put together, describe the full arc of romantic relationships: from first sight and hope-filled flirtation through doubt and betrayal, rage and reconciliation, passion and disappointment, and on to resolution (or resignation) and reminiscence. The best Old Boyfriend/Old Girlfriend lists are drawn from a number of romances, from your first love object up to and including the current one—or your next.

BOOK OF DREAMS, Bruce Springsteen
BOY FROM NEW YORK CITY, the Ad Libs
COLD KISSES, Richard Thompson
DIMMING OF THE DAY, Richard Thompson
DO RIGHT WOMAN—DO RIGHT MAN, Aretha Franklin
I ONLY WANT TO BE WITH YOU, Nicolette Larson
IF I NEEDED SOMEONE, Beatles
IF I NEEDED YOU, Townes Van Zandt
IN MY LIFE, Beatles
I'LL BE YOUR BABY TONIGHT, Bob Dylan
INTO THE MYSTIC, Van Morrison
LOSE AGAIN, Karla Bonoff
LOVE HAS NO PRIDE, Bonnie Raitt
LOVE MINUS ZERO/NO LIMIT, Bob Dylan
LOW SPARK OF HIGH-HEELED BOYS, Traffic
REASON TO BELIEVE, Tim Hardin
THE SHOOP SHOOP SONG (IT'S IN HIS KISS), Betty Everett
YOU CAN LEAVE YOUR HAT ON, Randy Newman

—MB

Breakup Therapy

Pull up a chair, and let yourself have a little cry. You'll start feeling better soon.

PENITENT, Suzanne Vega
I CAN'T MAKE YOU LOVE ME, Bonnie Raitt
HERE COME THOSE TEARS AGAIN, Jackson Browne
I DIDN'T UNDERSTAND, Elliott Smith
BAD LIVER AND A BROKEN HEART, Tom Waits
I KNOW IT'S OVER, the Smiths
THE GHOST OF YOU WALKS, Richard Thompson
ONLY A FOOL BREAKS HIS OWN HEART, Nick Lowe
FAMOUS BLUE RAINCOAT, Leonard Cohen
HARDER NOW THAT IT'S OVER, Ryan Adams
THE LAST NIGHT, Bob Mould

—KReichstein

Depressing Teen
Breakup Songs
of the New Millennium

Being a teenager in love can be terribly complicated, but it gets even worse when the breakup comes around. Here's one teen's playlist for soaking in the tub and crying over that lost love.

EITHER WAY, Guster
AND THEN YOU KISSED ME, the Cardigans
I'M LOST WITHOUT YOU, Blink-182
MY HAPPY ENDING, Avril Lavigne
THE SCIENTIST, Coldplay
IF I AIN'T GOT YOU, Alicia Keys
I DARE YOU TO MOVE, Switchfoot
LA CIENEGA JUST SMILED, Ryan Adams
BLUE, Lucinda Williams
MAD WORLD, Gary Jules
BACK AT ONE, Brian McKnight
PSYCHOBABBLE, Frou Frou
IRIS, the Goo Goo Dolls
SHE WILL BE LOVED, Maroon 5
TILL I GET OVER YOU, Michelle Branch
HOLD ON, Good Charlotte
PARADISE, Vanessa Carlton
THE REASON, Hoobastank
NOT PRETTY ENOUGH, Kasey Chambers
MY DECEMBER, Linkin Park
MY IMMORTAL, Evanescence

—LL

David Bowie

With his fearless mix of rebellion and entertainment, inventive lyrics, and drive to explore new styles, David Bowie has pushed pop-music culture for more than 30 years. Here, distilled down to ten songs, is Essential Bowie.

DIAMOND DOGS
THE MAN WHO SOLD THE WORLD
HEROES
AMSTERDAM
LITTLE DRUMMER BOY (with Bing Crosby)
FIVE YEARS
YOUNG AMERICANS
HANG ON TO YOURSELF
CRACKED ACTOR
UNDER PRESSURE (with Queen)

—TB

Songs for Your High-School Graduation Party

You've rented the motel room at the beach. You've got your iPod hooked up to your portable CD player, and the pizza guy is almost here. Why not celebrate your last day of high school with some of the tunes you've been listening to since freshman year?

A THOUSAND MILES, Vanessa Carlton
ALL YOU WANTED, Michelle Branch
BEAUTIFUL, Christina Aguilera
BURN, Usher
BYE BYE BYE, *NSync
CAN'T GET YOU OUT OF MY HEAD, Kylie Minogue
COMPLICATED, Avril Lavigne
COUNTRY GRAMMAR, Nelly
DANGEROUSLY IN LOVE, Beyonce
DESERT ROSE, Sting
DRIFT AWAY, Uncle Kracker
EVERY MORNING, Sugar Ray
GET THE PARTY STARTED, Pink
HERO, Enrique Iglesias
HEY BABY, No Doubt
HEY YA, OutKast
IN DA CLUB, 50 Cent
INDEPENDENT WOMEN, PART 1, Destiny's Child
LOSE YOURSELF, Eminem
PICTURE, Kid Rock and Sheryl Crow
THE FIRST CUT IS THE DEEPEST, Sheryl Crow
THE REASON, Hoobastank
THERE SHE GOES, Sixpence None the Richer

TOXIC, Britney Spears
UNWELL, Matchbox Twenty
WHENEVER, WHEREVER, Shakira
WHERE IS THE LOVE? Black Eyed Peas featuring Justin Timberlake
WORK IT, Missy Elliott
YOUR BODY IS A WONDERLAND, John Mayer

—MHamilton

Songs for Your 10th
High-School Reunion

It wasn't that long ago.

ACHY BREAKY HEART, Billy Ray Cyrus

ALL STAR, Smash Mouth

ALL THE SMALL THINGS, Blink-182

ALWAYS BE MY BABY, Mariah Carey

ANGEL, Sarah McLachlan

BABY GOT BACK, Sir Mix-A-Lot

BABY ONE MORE TIME, Britney Spears

BLACK OR WHITE, Michael Jackson

CALIFORNIA LOVE, 2Pac

CAN YOU FEEL THE LOVE TONIGHT? Elton John

DON'T LET GO (LOVE), En Vogue

DON'T SPEAK, No Doubt

DREAMING OF YOU, Selena

END OF THE ROAD, Boyz II Men

EVERYDAY IS A WINDING ROAD, Sheryl Crow

(EVERYTHING I DO) I DO IT FOR YOU, Bryan Adams

FIELDS OF GOLD, Sting

FREE FALLIN', Tom Petty & the Heartbreakers

GHETTO SUPASTAR, Pras Michel

GOOD RIDDANCE (TIME OF YOUR LIFE), Green Day

HOLD MY HAND, Hootie & the Blowfish

I CAN'T MAKE YOU LOVE ME, Bonnie Raitt

I SWEAR, All-4-One

I WILL ALWAYS LOVE YOU, Whitney Houston

I'LL BE MISSING YOU, Puff Daddy and the Family featuring Faith Evans

ICE ICE BABY, Vanilla Ice

IRIS, Goo Goo Dolls

IRONIC, Alanis Morissette

IT MUST HAVE BEEN LOVE, Roxette

LIVIN' LA VIDA LOCA, Ricky Martin

LOSING MY RELIGION, R.E.M.

LOVE WILL NEVER DO (WITHOUT YOU), Janet Jackson

MEN IN BLACK, Will Smith

MMM BOP, Hanson

MO MONEY, MO PROBLEMS, Notorious B.I.G. featuring Puff Daddy & Mase

MY HEART WILL GO ON, Celine Dion

NO RAIN, Blind Melon

ONE SWEET DAY, Mariah Carey and Boyz II Men

ONE WEEK, Barenaked Ladies

PATIENCE, Guns N' Roses

QUIT PLAYIN' GAMES WITH MY HEART, Backstreet Boys

SAVE THE BEST FOR LAST, Vanessa Williams

SHOW ME LOVE, Robyn

SMELLS LIKE TEEN SPIRIT, Nirvana

SMOOTH, Santana featuring Rob Thomas

STAY (I MISSED YOU), Lisa Loeb

TEARS IN HEAVEN, Eric Clapton

THE SIGN, Ace of Base

THIS KISS, Faith Hill

TRULY MADLY DEEPLY, Savage Garden

U CAN'T TOUCH THIS, MC Hammer

UN-BREAK MY HEART, Toni Braxton

UNDER THE BRIDGE, Red Hot Chili Peppers

WALK THIS WAY, Run DMC and Aerosmith

WATERFALLS, TLC

WHAT A MAN, Salt-N-Pepa featuring En Vogue

YOU WERE MEANT FOR ME, Jewel

YOU'RE STILL THE ONE, Shania Twain

—MHamilton

Songs for Your 20th
High-School Reunion

The mid-'80s was kind of a giddy period. This can partly be ascribed to the fashion sense at the time, when well-dressed men wore styling mousse, cultivated facial stubble, and slipped on loafers with no socks.

AGAINST ALL ODDS, Phil Collins
ALL NIGHT LONG (ALL NIGHT), Lionel Richie
BETTE DAVIS EYES, Kim Carnes
BILLIE JEAN, Michael Jackson
BORN IN THE U.S.A., Bruce Springsteen
CALL ME, Blondie
CELEBRATION, Kool & the Gang
CENTERFOLD, the J. Geils Band
CRAZY LITTLE THING CALLED LOVE, Queen
DON'T DREAM IT'S OVER, Crowded House
DON'T YOU (FORGET ABOUT ME), Simple Minds
DOWN UNDER, Men at Work
EVERY BREATH YOU TAKE, the Police
EVERYBODY WANTS TO RULE THE WORLD, Tears for Fears
FAITH, George Michael
HOLIDAY, Madonna
HUNGRY LIKE THE WOLF, Duran Duran
I LOVE ROCK 'N' ROLL, Joan Jett & the Blackhearts
I MELT WITH YOU, Modern English
IN YOUR EYES, Peter Gabriel
JACK AND DIANE, John Mellencamp
JESSIE'S GIRL, Rick Springfield
JUMP, Van Halen
KARMA CHAMELEON, Culture Club
LIVIN' ON A PRAYER, Bon Jovi
LOVE IS A BATTLEFIELD, Pat Benatar
LOVE SHACK, the B-52's
MANIC MONDAY, Bangles

MY BEST FRIEND'S GIRL, the Cars
1984, Eurythmics
NOTHIN' BUT A GOOD TIME, Poison
OPEN ARMS, Journey
PHYSICAL, Olivia Newton-John
POUR SOME SUGAR ON ME, Def Leppard
RAPPER'S DELIGHT, the Sugarhill Gang
RELAX, Frankie Goes to Hollywood
SUMMER OF '69, Bryan Adams
SUPER FREAK, Rick James
SWEET DREAMS (ARE MADE OF THIS), Eurythmics
TAKE MY BREATH AWAY, Berlin
TAKE ON ME, A-Ha
TOTAL ECLIPSE OF THE HEART, Bonnie Tyler
WE GOT THE BEAT, the Go-Go's
WHAT I LIKE ABOUT YOU, the Romantics
WHAT'S LOVE GOT TO DO WITH IT, Tina Turner
WHEN DOVES CRY, Prince
WHIP IT, Devo
WHITE WEDDING, Billy Idol
WITH OR WITHOUT YOU, U2
YOU SHOOK ME ALL NIGHT LONG, AC/DC

—MHamilton

Songs for Your 30th
High-School Reunion

A list of songs to listen to before your 30th reunion, and not one of them is from Peter Frampton.

AMERICAN PIE, Don McLean
ANGIE, Rolling Stones
BETH, Kiss
BOHEMIAN RHAPSODY, Queen
BORN TO RUN, Bruce Springsteen
DANCING QUEEN, ABBA
DISCO INFERNO, the Trammps
DON'T FEAR THE REAPER, Blue Oyster Cult
DREAM ON, Aerosmith
EVERYBODY PLAYS THE FOOL, the Main Ingredient
EVERYDAY PEOPLE, Sly & the Family Stone
FIRE AND RAIN, James Taylor
GET DOWN TONIGHT, KC & the Sunshine Band
GO YOUR OWN WAY, Fleetwood Mac
HOTEL CALIFORNIA, Eagles
I GOT A NAME, Jim Croce
I WANT YOU BACK, the Jackson 5
I WILL SURVIVE, Gloria Gaynor
I'LL BE AROUND, the Spinners
IMAGINE, John Lennon
IT'S TOO LATE, Carole King
JOY TO THE WORLD, Three Dog Night
LET'S STAY TOGETHER, Al Green
LISTEN TO THE MUSIC, Doobie Brothers
LOVE TRAIN, the O'Jays
MAGGIE MAY, Rod Stewart
MANDY, Barry Manilow
MIDNIGHT TRAIN TO GEORGIA, Gladys Knight & the Pips
MORE THAN A FEELING, Boston

NIGHT FEVER, Bee Gees
NIGHT MOVES, Bob Seger & the Silver Bullet Band
PIANO MAN, Billy Joel
REELIN' IN THE YEARS, Steely Dan
ROCKET MAN, Elton John
SATURDAY IN THE PARK, Chicago
SEASONS IN THE SUN, Terry Jacks
SEPTEMBER, Earth, Wind & Fire
STAIRWAY TO HEAVEN, Led Zeppelin
STAYIN' ALIVE, Bee Gees
SUNDOWN, Gordon Lightfoot
SUPERSTITION, Stevie Wonder
SWEET CAROLINE, Neil Diamond
SWEET HOME ALABAMA, Lynyrd Skynyrd
TAKE ME HOME, COUNTRY ROADS, John Denver
THE JOKER, the Steve Miller Band
THE THEME FROM SHAFT, Isaac Hayes
(THEY LONG TO BE) CLOSE TO YOU, Carpenters
WHAT'S GOING ON, Marvin Gaye
YOU MAKE ME FEEL BRAND NEW, the Stylistics

—MHamilton

Songs for Your 40th
High-School Reunion

Although it may resemble the playlist from a Boss Radio AM station, it's actually a list of songs to prepare you for your 40th reunion.

BABY, I NEED YOUR LOVING, the Four Tops

BORN TO BE WILD, Steppenwolf

BROWN EYED GIRL, Van Morrison

CALIFORNIA DREAMIN', the Mamas & the Papas

GOOD LOVIN', the Rascals

GOOD VIBRATIONS, the Beach Boys

HAPPY TOGETHER, the Turtles

HELP! the Beatles

HEY JUDE, the Beatles

HONKY TONK WOMEN, Rolling Stones

(I CAN'T GET NO) SATISFACTION, the Rolling Stones

I GOT YOU (I FEEL GOOD), James Brown

I GOT YOU BABE, Sonny & Cher

I HEARD IT THROUGH THE GRAPEVINE, Marvin Gaye

I'M A BELIEVER, the Monkees

LIGHT MY FIRE, the Doors

ME AND BOBBY MCGEE, Janis Joplin

MRS. ROBINSON, Simon & Garfunkel

MY GENERATION, the Who

MY GIRL, the Temptations

PENNY LANE, the Beatles

PROUD MARY, Creedence Clearwater Revival

PURPLE HAZE, Jimi Hendrix

RESPECT, Aretha Franklin

SOMEBODY TO LOVE, Jefferson Airplane

TEARS OF A CLOWN, Smokey Robinson & the Miracles

TIME OF THE SEASON, the Zombies

UNCHAINED MELODY, the Righteous Brothers

WHEN A MAN LOVES A WOMAN, Percy Sledge
WHERE DID OUR LOVE GO, Diana Ross & the Supremes
WILD THING, the Troggs
YOU CAN'T HURRY LOVE, Diana Ross & the Supremes
YOU REALLY GOT ME, the Kinks
(YOUR LOVE KEEPS LIFTING ME) HIGHER AND HIGHER, Jackie Wilson
YOU'VE LOST THAT LOVIN' FEELIN', the Righteous Brothers

—MHamilton

Songs for Your 50th
High-School Reunion

The United States conducted its first underground nuclear test in 1957, but things were already popping aboveground.

ALL I HAVE TO DO IS DREAM, the Everly Brothers
BE MY BABY, the Ronettes
BELIEVE WHAT YOU SAY, Ricky Nelson
BLUEBERRY HILL, Fats Domino
CHANTILLY LACE, the Big Bopper
COME GO WITH ME, the Del Vikings
DA DOO RON RON, the Crystals
DO YOU LOVE ME?, the Contours
DUKE OF EARL, Gene Chandler
GREAT BALLS OF FIRE, Jerry Lee Lewis
HOUND DOG, Elvis Presley
I FOUGHT THE LAW, the Bobby Fuller Four
IN THE STILL OF THE NIGHT, the Five Satins
JAILHOUSE ROCK, Elvis Presley
JOHNNY B. GOODE, Chuck Berry
LA BAMBA, Ritchie Valens
LITTLE DARLIN', the Diamonds
MY BOYFRIEND'S BACK, the Angels
OH, PRETTY WOMAN, Roy Orbison
PEGGY SUE, Buddy Holly
ROCK AROUND THE CLOCK, Bill Haley & His Comets
RUNAROUND SUE, Dion
RUNAWAY, Del Shannon
SHERRY, Frankie Valli & the Four Seasons
STAND BY ME, Ben E. King
STAY, Maurice Williams & the Zodiacs
SUMMERTIME BLUES, Eddie Cochran
TEQUILA, the Champs

THE GREAT PRETENDER, the Platters
THE TWIST, Chubby Checker
TUTTI FRUTTI, Little Richard
TWISTIN' THE NIGHT AWAY, Sam Cooke
UNDER THE BOARDWALK, the Drifters
WILL YOU LOVE ME TOMORROW, the Shirelles
WONDERFUL WORLD, Sam Cooke

—MHamilton

Old-School Hip-Hop

The old-school period of hip-hop concerns the genre's first recording artists, those who released singles and albums between 1978 and 1984 (give or take a year, depending on who's counting). Most of the earliest songs were party anthems built around simple, oft-repeated samples, although artists such as Melle Mel and Spoonie Gee did eventually write darker lyrics concerning urban street life. Even if some of the tunes sound sonically dated, they have a naive enthusiasm that's addictive.

BASSLINE, Mantronix
EGYPT, EGYPT, the Egyptian Lover
KING TIM III, Fatback Band
LA DI DA DI, Doug E. Fresh
MONSTER JAM, Spoonie Gee and the Sequence
ONE FOR THE TREBLE, Davy DMX
ROXANNE, ROXANNE, UTFO
ROXANNE'S REVENGE, Roxanne Shanté
SHE'S FRESH, Rock Steady Crew
THAT'S THE JOINT, Funky 4 + 1
THE ADVENTURES OF GRANDMASTER FLASH ON THE WHEELS OF STEEL, Grandmaster Flash
THE MESSAGE, Grandmaster Flash & the Furious Five
RAPPER'S DELIGHT, Sugarhill Gang
PLANET ROCK, Afrika Bambaataa
THE BREAKS, Kurtis Blow
JAM ON REVENGE (THE WIKKI-WIKKI SONG), Newcleus
TO THE BEAT Y'ALL, Lady B
WHIP IT, Treacherous Three
WHITE LINES (DON'T DO IT), Melle Mel

—DS

Golden Age of
Hip-Hop

These songs are from the second wave of hip-hop, which took place roughly between 1984 and 1993 and is considered by many the high-water mark of the music. During this period, artists could be stridently political, musically inventive, and culturally important and still sell huge amounts of records. Or they could be raunchy, goofy, or silly and sell tons of records. Everything was allowed; nothing was forbidden.

BABY GOT BACK, Sir Mix-a-Lot
BUST A MOVE, Young MC
CHILDREN'S STORY, Slick Rick
FIGHT THE POWER, Public Enemy
INSANE IN THE BRAIN, Cypress Hill
IT'S TRICKY, Run-DMC
JUMP AROUND, House of Pain
JUST A FRIEND, Biz Markie
LADIES FIRST, Queen Latifah
MAMA SAID KNOCK YOU OUT, LL Cool J
ME, MYSELF, AND I, De La Soul
O.P.P., Naughty By Nature
PAID IN FULL, Eric B. & Rakim
PUSH IT, Salt-N-Pepa
RAW, Big Daddy Kane
SCENARIO, A Tribe Called Quest
STOP THE VIOLENCE, Boogie Down Productions
SURE SHOT, Beastie Boys
THEY REMINISCE OVER YOU, Pete Rock & C.L. Smooth
TRIBE VIBES, Jungle Brothers
WILD THING, Tone Loc
WORDS I MANIFEST, Gang Starr

—DS

Gangsta Rap

Public Enemy's leader Chuck D once called hip-hop "black people's CNN." The subgenre of gangsta rap certainly plays like documentary news, depicting the inner workings of pimps, drug dealers, and gangbangers. While this view of the urban experience may not be prevalent, it's definitely valid—and, in the hands of these artists, visceral and disturbing.

BORN AND RAISED IN COMPTON, DJ Quik
BOYZ-N-THE HOOD, Eazy-E
CALIFORNIA LOVE, Tupac
COLORS, Ice-T
DAMN IT FEELS GOOD TO BE A GANGSTA, Geto Boys
DEAD HOMIEZ, Ice Cube
DEAD MEN TELL NO LIES, Compton's Most Wanted
GANGSTA GANGSTA, NWA
GANGSTA'S PARADISE, Coolio
GIN AND JUICE, Snoop Dogg
GUERILLAS IN THA MIST, Da Lench Mob
MAKE EM SAY UGH, Master P
NEW YORK, NEW YORK, Tha Dogg Pound
NUTHIN' BUT A 'G' THANG, Dr. Dre
P.S.K. WHAT DOES IT MEAN?, Schoolly D
RAPPERS' BALL, E-40
READY TO DIE, the Notorious B.I.G.
REGULATE, Warren G
SHOOK ONES, PT. 2, Mobb Deep
SHORTY THE PIMP, Too $hort

—DS

That Funky Music:
Songs for Gettin' Down to a '70s Beat

While many in America in the 1970s danced to a sterilized disco beat, some stalwarts stuck to a purer, rawer style of dance music.

GIVE UP THE FUNK (TEAR THE ROOF OFF THE SUCKER), Parliament
LOVE ROLLERCOASTER, Ohio Players
MACHINE GUN, the Commodores
SERPENTINE FIRE, Earth, Wind & Fire
EARLY IN THE MORNING, the Gap Band
GET THE FUNK OUT MA FACE, the Brothers Johnson
WILL IT GO ROUND IN CIRCLES? Billy Preston
SPIRIT OF THE BOOGIE, Kool & the Gang
ATOMIC DOG, George Clinton
SUPERSTITION, Stevie Wonder

—DM

Soul Review

You've read Nick Hornby's *High Fidelity* (or seen the movie), and like Rob Gordon, you've decided that one of your dream jobs is to work for Atlantic Records in the '60s so that you can meet Aretha Franklin, Otis Redding, and other great artists who recorded for the label. Or maybe you just want good music for your next party. Either way, here's a list of songs from great '60s soul artists who made records for the Atlantic label or in the Stax studios that Atlantic often worked with.

A NATURAL WOMAN, Aretha Franklin

B-A-B-Y, Carla Thomas

BRING IT ON HOME TO ME, Otis Redding and Carla Thomas

CHAIN OF FOOLS, Aretha Franklin

DO RIGHT WOMAN—DO RIGHT MAN, Aretha Franklin

DR. FEELGOOD, Aretha Franklin

GOT TO GET YOU OFF MY MIND, Solomon Burke

GREEN ONIONS, Booker T. and the MG's

HOLD ON, I'M COMING, Sam and Dave

HOLD WHAT YOU GOT, Joe Tex

I NEVER LOVED A MAN (THE WAY I LOVE YOU), Aretha Franklin

IN THE MIDNIGHT HOUR, Wilson Pickett

I'VE BEEN LOVING YOU TOO LONG (TO STOP NOW), Otis Redding

KNOCK ON WOOD, Eddie Floyd

LAND OF 1000 DANCES, Wilson Pickett

LAST NIGHT, the Mar-Keys

MR. PITIFUL, Otis Redding

RESPECT, Aretha Franklin

SAVE ME, Aretha Franklin

(SITTIN' ON) THE DOCK OF THE BAY, Otis Redding

THAT'S HOW STRONG MY LOVE IS, Otis Redding

THINK, Aretha Franklin

WALKING THE DOG, Rufus Thomas

WHEN A MAN LOVES A WOMAN, Percy Sledge

YOU DON'T MISS YOUR WATER, William Bell

—CC

Marvin Gaye Duets

Through the '60s and into the '70s, Detroit's Motown record label paired its leading ladies man, Marvin Gaye, with a series of its female singers. The label shot off sparks when it teamed Gaye with Tammi Terrell, who together made some of Motown's most beautiful records.

ONCE UPON A TIME, Marvin Gaye and Mary Wells
WHAT'S THE MATTER WITH YOU, BABY, Marvin Gaye and Mary Wells
SO GOOD TO BE LOVED BY YOU, Marvin Gaye and Oma Page
IT'S GOT TO BE A MIRACLE (THIS THING CALLED LOVE), Marvin Gaye and Kim Weston
IT TAKES TWO, Marvin Gaye and Kim Weston
AIN'T NO MOUNTAIN HIGH ENOUGH, Marvin Gaye and Tammi Terrell
AIN'T NOTHING LIKE THE REAL THING, Marvin Gaye and Tammi Terrell
I'M YOUR PUPPET, Marvin Gaye and Tammi Terrell
IF I COULD BUILD MY WHOLE WORLD AROUND YOU, Marvin Gaye and Tammi Terrell
YOU'RE ALL I NEED TO GET BY, Marvin Gaye and Tammi Terrell
YOUR PRECIOUS LOVE, Marvin Gaye and Tammi Terrell
STOP, LOOK, LISTEN (TO YOUR HEART), Marvin Gaye and Diana Ross
YOU ARE EVERYTHING, Marvin Gaye and Diana Ross

—CC

Top-Secret Songs
to Pack a Dance Floor

I'm somewhat embarrassed to admit this now, but back in the 1980s and early 1990s, I was a keyboard player in a top-40 band that played all over Florida. Getting gigs at that time was pretty tough because there were a ton of bands and just a few hot clubs, but our band worked steady pretty much all year long because of one main advantage that we had over most of the other bands—we could absolutely pack the dance floor.

If you came to see us play, no matter what night it was, you could bet the dance floor would be jammin', and one of the reasons was that we had identified a bunch of songs that we could pull out at any time to literally make people rush the floor. Better yet, we learned how to stack these songs in a particular order that would keep the dance floor jammed the entire set, and club owners love a packed dance floor. It makes the club look hot, it makes the dancers hot, and they want more drinks to cool themselves down. It's a vicious cycle, but that's how we made our name in this market. Now, some of these songs we absolutely hated. We hated the songs, we hated hearing them, we hated playing them even more, but it's what we had to do to get the party started, so we smiled and danced and did our gig.

Here are just a few of those songs that were guaranteed to pack the floor in any club, on any night, no matter what:

GONNA MAKE YOU SWEAT, C+C Music Factory
WORD UP, Cameo
NO PARKING ON THE DANCE FLOOR, Midnight Star
YOU DROPPED A BOMB ON ME, Gap Band
HOT NUMBER/GET OFF, Foxy

BOOGIE OOGIE OOGIE, Taste of Honey
RING MY BELL, Anita Ward
WILD THING, Tone Loc
LOVE SHACK, B-52's
ICE ICE BABY, Vanilla Ice
CELEBRATION, Kool & the Gang
BRICK HOUSE, the Commodores
PLAY THAT FUNKY MUSIC, Wild Cherry
YMCA, Village People
LE FREAK, Chic
SUPER FREAK, Rick James
LAST DANCE, Donna Summer
BILLIE JEAN, Michael Jackson
WHAT I LIKE ABOUT YOU, the Romantics
ADDICTED TO LOVE, Robert Palmer
RELAX, Frankie Goes to Hollywood

—SK

Almost Opera

If you don't feel like putting up with opera but still want to revel in the sound of a glorious voice surrounded by a sumptuous orchestra, this is the list for you—a dozen, to fit any mood.

FOUR LAST SONGS, Richard Strauss, sung by Gundula Janowitz with Herbert von Karajan and the Berlin Philharmonic (DG/Galleria). Heavenly bliss set to music. If you're skeptical, listen to the third song, "Beim Schlafengehen." You'll never be the same again. (Alternate take: Lucia Popp and Klaus Tennstedt on EMI.)

WESENDONK LEIDER, Richard Wagner, sung by Christa Ludwig (EMI). Both Kirsten Flagstad and Tiana Lemnitz have sensational historic recordings (various labels).

INGEMISCO from "Messa da Requiem," by Giuseppe Verdi, sung by Jussi Björling (Decca).

LIBERA ME from "Messa da Requiem," by Giuseppe Verdi, sung by Leontyne Price (Decca).

AH, PERFIDO! Ludwig van Beethoven, sung by Birgit Nilsson (Testament).

LET THE BRIGHT SERAPHIM from "Samson," by G. F. Handel, sung by Joan Sutherland (Decca).

ICH BIN DER WELT ABHANDEN GEKOMMEN from "5 Rückertlieder," by Gustav Mahler, sung by Janet Baker (EMI). Christa Ludwig also has a superb recording on DG.

IN TRUTINA from "Carmina Burana," by Carl Orff, sung by Barbara Bonney (Decca). The eternal feminine in all its sweet seductiveness.

CIRCA MEA PECTORA from "Carmina Burana," by Carl Orff, sung by Simon Keenlyside (DG).

EXSULTATE, JUBILATE, W. A. Mozart, sung by Kiri Te Kanawa (Philips).

VORREI SPIEGARVI, O DIO! W. A. Mozart, sung by Edita Gruberova (Teldec).

CÄCILIE and **ZUEIGNUNG,** Richard Strauss, sung by Montserrat Caballe (DG/Galleria).

—PT

Curses, Vengeance, and Evil Doings: A Little List of Operatic Nastiness

Opera is chock-full of people who are ... well, not nice. They plot evil deeds, wreak vengeance, and put curses on the good folks. All of which tends to make opera *lots* of fun.

ENTWEIHTE GÖTTER! from Act 2 of Wagner's *Lohengrin*
The sorceress Ortrud calling on her pagan gods to aid her treachery against the upstart Christians. Before listening to Christa Ludwig (EMI), make sure any loose objects around you are tied down.

SI, PEL CIEL from the end of Act 2 of Verdi's *Otello*
Placido Domingo (Otello) and Sherrill Milnes (Iago) swearing vengeance on poor, innocent Desdemona and Cassio (RCA). Chilling.

VA, LA MORTE SUL CAPO TI PENDE from the end of Act 2 of Donizetti's *Roberto Devereux*
A furious Beverly Sills as Queen Elizabeth I signs the death warrant for her beloved Earl of Essex and throws him into the Tower (DG). It's Bette Davis with high notes letting fly at Errol Flynn.

DER HÖLLE RACHE from Act 2 of Mozart's *Die Zauberflöte*
Rita Streich (DG) as the Queen of the Night proclaiming her heart is "seething with hellish vengeance"—complete with high Fs above high C. Don't try this one in the shower.

O DON FATALE from Act 4 of Verdi's Don Carlos
Shirley Verrett (EMI) as Princess Eboli cursing her beauty that has gotten her into one hell of a mess.

HELLE WEHR! HEILIGE WAFFE! from Act 2 of Wagner's
Götterdämmerung
A furious Brünnhilde swears on Hagen's spear in front of all the vassals that Siegfried is lying. Birgit Nilsson's performance (Decca) is the stuff of which legends are made.

D'ORESTE, D'AIACE from Act 3 of Mozart's *Idomeneo*
Electra losing it big time and spinning out of control. Carol Vaness (DG) is the clear choice here.

A LUI VIVO, LA TOMBA from Act 4 of Verdi's *Aida*
Princess Amneris cursing the priests who have just sentenced the man she loves to be buried alive. You don't have to speak Italian to know *exactly* what Giulietta Simionato (Decca) is saying.

HA, WELCH' EIN AUGENBLICK from Act 1 of Beethoven's *Fidelio*
The evil Pizarro plots his wickedness. Dietrich Fischer-Dieskau (DG) is the modern choice, but if you can do without stereo for 4 minutes, listen to Friedrich Schorr's 1922 recording on Preiser's Lebendige Vergangenheit label. It's still the standard against which all other Pizarros are measured.

—PT

"I Think I'm Losing My Mind ..."

One reason why mad scenes are so popular in opera is that an insane character allows composers the opportunity to push the boundaries of vocal limitations—to *really* go over the top. Singers love doing them, audiences love hearing them, and singers especially love hearing audiences roaring their approval when it's all over.

LUCIA'S MAD SCENE from Act 3 of Donizetti's Lucia di Lammermoor
Poor Lucy of Ravenswood Castle, what's a girl to do but sing the most famous mad scene in all of opera? Joan Sutherland (Decca) was labeled by the Italians (who know a thing or two about mad scenes) as "La Stupenda" for good reason. For a legendary live performance, check out "The Berlin Lucia," Maria Callas in Berlin, 1955 (on a variety of labels)—the Berliners sound like a bunch of South Americans in the closing moments of an important soccer match.

Britten's **PETER GRIMES**
One of the few genuine mad scenes for a male singer is in *Peter Grimes*. Jon Vickers (Philips) makes Grimes's unraveling while wading into the ocean to drown almost unbearable. It's one of the truly great, haunting moments in all of opera.

FINAL SCENE of Richard Strauss's *Salome*
Oscar Wilde turned the biblical story into a Freudian tour de force, and Strauss's music heightens the emotions as an unhinged teenage girl spends 15 minutes caressing and kissing the severed head of John the Baptist that's been plopped on a silver platter at her request. The part might have been written for Ljuba Welitsch (Sony). No one since has equaled the Bulgarian Bombshell in the role.

L'ALTRA NOTTE IN FONDO AL MARE from Act 3 of Boito's *Mefistofele*
Based on Goethe's *Faust*, this is Margherita languishing in prison. Renata Tebaldi (Decca) shows why this was one of her best roles. Claudio Muzio's 1935 recording of the aria (various labels) is one of the great vocal recordings of all time.

QUI LA VOCE ... VIEN, DILETTO from Act 2 of Bellini's *I Puritani*
How an opera about a bunch of Puritans could give the world one of
the most sensual, beautiful melodies ever written is a mystery. But it's
no mystery why Maria Callas's very first recording in 1949 (on Gala
and many other labels) immediately made her famous. Joan
Sutherland (Decca) also dazzles as the mad Elvira.

A VOS JEUX MES AMIS, Ophélie's Mad Scene from Act IV
of Thomas's *Hamlet*
Yes, it's true—a 19th-century Frenchman wrote an opera based on
Shakespeare's sacred play. Natalie Dessay (EMI) is utterly enchanting
while vividly demonstrating why this opera was so immensely popular
in its day.

UNA MACCHIA È QUI TUTTORA, Lady Macbeth's Sleepwalking Scene
from Act 4 of Verdi's *Macbeth*
The first of Verdi's three Shakespearean operas, and one that has challenged great singing actresses for over 150 years. Leonie Rysanek (RCA)
and Maria Callas (EMI) made it their own. So did Martha Mödl
(Preiser), even singing it in German as "Dieser Flecken kommt immer
wieder."

—PT

"It Ain't Over Until ..."

The old joke about "It ain't over until the fat lady sings" is certainly true in opera, regardless of the size of the singer. Historically, operatic composers were men of the theater, and so they knew how to save the best for last (or close to it), so that the audience's evening would end ... well, on a high note—metaphorically if not literally. Here are some examples.

STARKE SCHEITE from the end of Wagner's *Götterdämmerung*
This isn't just the end of Wagner's 5-hour opera, it's also the end of his gargantuan four-evening epic, *The Ring of the Nibelung*, all about the creation, destruction, and rebirth of the world. Wagner successfully summed it all up in this piece, also known as "Brünnhilde's Immolation Scene." Birgit Nilsson (Decca) will make you a true believer. Astrid Varnay (Testament) and Kirsten Flagstad (Nimbus) are spectacular, too.

OH! S'IO POTESSI, the final scene of Donizetti's *Il Pirata*
Listening to Maria Callas (EMI) will explain why she has the reputation she does. Montserrat Caballe (RCA) will do the same.

TANTI AFFETTI, from the end of Rossini's *La Donna del Lago*
The reason this opera faded into the woodwork for a century or so is very simple—no one could sing it properly. Then along came Marilyn Horne (Decca), with her rich, gorgeous mezzo voice, effortless two-octave jumps, lightning-fast even scale passages, and perfect trill, and—voilà. The Rossini Foundation in Italy (justifiably) named her the greatest singer in the world.

GIVE ME MY ROBE, Cleopatra's death scene from Barber's *Anthony and Cleopatra*
Leontyne Price (RCA) opened the new Metropolitan Opera House at Lincoln Center in the world premiere of this opera. This is the one scene everyone loved, and with very good reason.

VATER, BIST DU? the Empress's transformation scene from Act 3 of Richard Strauss's *Die Frau ohne Schatten*

The most ambitious—and greatest—of all Strauss's operas, *The Woman Without a Shadow* only became popular the last 40 years or so. That was largely because the great Leonie Rysanek began singing the role of the Empress. The early recording is on Decca; the stereo is on DG. Both are treats.

MARTEN ALLER ARTEN, from Mozart's
The Abduction from the Seraglio
Constanze has been captured by Turkish pirates and is being held in the Pasha's seraglio. Here she explains—in considerable detail and with great emotion—the tortures she is willing to endure to remain faithful to her True Love. Eleanor Steber (RCA) sings it like no one else.

NON HAN CALMA LE MIE PENE from Graun's *Montezuma*
As sung by Joan Sutherland (Decca), Eupaforice's aria from this 18th-century opera has to be the most lavishly embellished aria ever recorded—even though Sutherland makes it sound as easy to sing as "Row, row, row your boat." Simply astonishing and mesmerizing.

MORGAN MITTAG UM ELF, the final scene from
Richard Strauss's *Capriccio*
The Countess suddenly realizes she must choose between two suitors the next morning. Strauss, who was in his 80s, knew that *Capriccio* would be his final opera, and he used this last, great scene for soprano and orchestra to bid farewell to his beloved art form. Elisabeth Schwarzkopf's 1953 recording (EMI) of just the final scene will have you puddling up and sniffling your nose all weekend.

—PT

Movie Music:
Classical

Savvy film directors know the value of a good score: The continuity of music helps to counterbalance the frequent cuts in modern film editing. Ideally, each movie would have an original score, composed to suit the unique characteristics of the film's mood and story. But life is short and budgets are tight, and rather than expend the energy and money to find a composer who will write The Perfect Score and bring it in on time and under budget, many directors turn to the vast corpus of high-quality (and often copyright-free) classical music of the past.

ADAGIO FOR STRINGS (ARRANGED FROM THE STRING QUARTET, OP. 11), Samuel Barber
Platoon, Lorenzo's Oil
From *Great Performances: Barber's Adagio and Other Romantic Favorites for Strings.* The New York Philharmonic, Leonard Bernstein conducting. Sony 38484

SYMPHONY NO. 9 IN D MINOR, OP. 125, CHORAL, IV: PRESTO; ALLEGRO ASSAI ODE TO JOY, Ludwig van Beethoven
Die Hard, A Clockwork Orange
From *Beethoven: Symphony No. 9 "Choral."* The Boston Symphony Orchestra, Erich Leinsdorf conducting. RCA 7880.

MINUET FROM STRING QUINTET IN E MAJOR, OP. 11 NO. 5, Luigi Boccherini
The Ladykillers (1955 and 2004 versions), *Greystoke—the Legend of Tarzan, The Hudsucker Proxy*
From *Boccherini: String Quintets, Minuet in A.* Europa Galante. Virgin Classics (Veritas) 5454212.

CLAIR DE LUNE, FROM SUITE BERGAMASQUE FOR SOLO PIANO, Claude Debussy
Ocean's Eleven, Frankie and Johnny, The Right Stuff, Down and Out in Beverly Hills
From *Debussy: Clair de Lune & Other Piano Works.* lexis Weissenberg, piano. Deutsche Grammophon 445547.

DÔME ÉPAIS LE JASMIN À LA ROSE S'ASSEMBLE (FLOWER DUET), FROM THE OPERA LAKMÉ, Léo Delibes
The Hunger, I've Heard the Mermaids Singing, Meet the Parents, True Romance, Someone to Watch over Me
From *Great Recordings of the Century: Delibes, Lakmé.* Mady Mesplé & Danielle Millet, with the Chorus and Orchestra of the Théâtre National de L'Opéra-Comique, Alain Lombard conducting. EMI Classics 7243 5 67742 2 3

RHAPSODY IN BLUE FOR PIANO AND ORCHESTRA, George Gershwin
Manhattan
From *The Bernstein Century: Gershwin.* The Columbia Symphony Orchestra & Leonard Bernstein, pianist and conductor. Sony 63086.

SINFONY FROM SOLOMON (ARRIVAL OF THE QUEEN OF SHEBA), George Frideric Handel
Four Weddings and a Funeral, Heartburn, Forces of Nature
From *Handel: Solomon,* Gabrieli Consort and Players, Paul McCreesh conducting. Deutsche Grammophon Gesellschaft (Archiv Produktion) 459 688-2.

SYMPHONY NO. 5 IN C-SHARP MINOR, IV: ADAGIETTO (SEHR LANGSAM), Gustav Mahler
Death in Venice, Lorenzo's Oil, Timecode
From *Great Recordings of the Century: Mahler, Symphony No. 5.* New Philharmonia Orchestra, Sir John Barbirolli conducting. EMI Classics 7243 5 66910 2 5.

—VG

Renaissance:
Choral Music

Although you wouldn't know it from most college survey classes and PBS documentaries, the Renaissance produced composers who were every bit the equal of Michelangelo, Dürer, and Shakespeare in artistic achievement. Working for the most part at court and chapel, these musicians developed the technique of purely vocal counterpoint to a high art (as the 16th century progressed, however, instruments began to be welcomed into the mix, as the Gabrieli example shows). The continental composers aimed for a sound balanced from top to bottom, with no single voice taking priority. The interaction among the voices was governed by the ideals of order and restraint—classic in the purest sense of the word. On the other hand, it will come as no surprise to learn that the English, in their delightfully eccentric way, felt less need of balance or restraint. Taverner's work in particular is marked by an exuberant flamboyance that is more late Gothic in spirit. But all of these composers share one thing in common: faith in the primacy of the human voice as the perfect vehicle for music.

AVE MARIA, Josquin Desprez
From *Josquin: Missa L'homme armé,* Oxford Camerata; Jeremy Summerly, conducting. Naxos 8.553428.

ÉLÉGIE SUR LA MORT DE JOSQUIN: MUSAE JOVIS À 6 VOIX (ELEGY ON THE DEATH OF JOSQUIN), Nicolas Gombert
From *Heavenly Spheres,* Le Studio de Musique Ancienne de Montréal; Christopher Jackson, director. CBC Enterprises 1121.

MISSA GLORIA TIBI TRINITAS, John Taverner
From *John Taverner: Missa Gloria Tibi Trinitas,* the Tallis Scholars; Peter Phillips, conducting. Gimell Records CDGIM 004.

LAMENTATIONS OF JEREMIAH (LAMENTATIO JEREMIAE), Thomas Tallis
From *Thomas Tallis: The Lamentations of Jeremiah,* the Hilliard Ensemble; Paul Hillier, conducting. ECM Records 21341.

MASS FOR 4 VOICES, William Byrd
From *The William Byrd Edition, Vol. 5: The Masses,* the Cardinall's
Musick; Andrew Carwood, conducting. ASV Gaudeamus CD GAU206.

MISSA PAPAE MARCELLI, Giovanni Luigi da Palestrina
From *Palestrina: Missa Papae Marcelli & Allegri: Miserere,* Westminster
Abbey Cathedral Choir; Simon Preston, conducting.
Archiv Produktion 415517.

OSCULETUR ME, Orlandus Lassus
From *Orlandus Lassus: Missa Osculetur me,* the Tallis Scholars; directed
by Peter Phillips. Gimell Records CDGIM 018.

O MAGNUM MYSTERIUM, Tomás Luis da Victoria
From *Victoria: O Magnum Mysterium; Ascendens Christus in altum,*
Choir of Westminster Cathedral; David Hill, Master of the Music.
Hyperion CDA66190.

IN ECCLESIIS, Giovanni Gabrieli
From *Venetian Church Music,* Taverner Consort, Choir & Players;
Andrew Parrott, conducting. Virgin Classics (Veritas) 5619342.

—VG

Baroque:
Instrumental Music

Instrumental music only came into its own as a distinct genre in the 17th century; before that, instrumentalists played (for the most part) vocal music or pieces that sounded like vocal music. But around 1600, instrumental music began to shake off its vocal ancestry, and a new breed of virtuoso performers set about the task of creating styles of music that would exploit the full capacities of their particular instrument. This, in turn, led to the rise of the first great instrument builders—virtuosos in their own right: Stradivarius (the violin family), the Ruckers dynasty (harpsichords), Schitger (organs), and later, Hotteterre (woodwinds). This list does not try to present the "Greatest Instrumental Works of the Baroque" (whatever that could possibly mean). It is merely an attempt to provide an introduction to the dazzling variety and richness of the instrumental music of the 17th and 18th centuries.

PRÉLUDE TO THE TE DEUM, Marc-Antoine Charpentier
From *Charpentier: Te Deum,* Les Arts Florissants; William Christie, conducting. Harmonia Mundi 601298.

TOMBEAU DE MEZANGEAU, Ennemond Gaultier
From *Piéces de Luth du Vieux Gaultier;* Hopkinson Smith, lute.
Astrée E 8703.

SUITE IN F MAJOR FOR HARPSICHORD, Louis Couperin
From *The Bauyn Manuscript: Harpsichord Music at the Court of Louis XIV;* Byron Schenkman, harpsichord. Wild Boar WLBR 9603.

FOLIES D'ESPAGNE, Marin Marais
From *Marin Marais: Piéces de Viole du Second Livre (1701);* Jordi Savall, bass viol; Anne Gallet, harpsichord; Hopkinson Smith, theorbo. Astrée Musica Gallica E 7770.

BRANDENBURG CONCERTO NO. 5 FOR HARPSICHORD, FLUTE, VIOLIN, AND STRINGS, J. S. Bach
From *J. S. Bach: The Brandenburg Concertos*; Gustav Leonhardt, harpsichord; Sigiswald Kuijken, violin; Barthold Kuijken, flute; Anner Bylsma, cello; Gustav Leonhardt, conducting. Sony SB2K 62946.

SONATA FOR TRUMPET, STRINGS, AND CONTINUO IN D MAJOR, Henry Purcell
From *Purcell: Ode for St. Cecilia's Day*; David Staff, trumpet, and the Orchestra of the Golden Age; Robert Glenton, conducting. Naxos Classical 8.553444.

PASSAGALIA FOR SOLO VIOLIN, Biber
From *Die Rosencranz-Sonaten*; John Holloway, violin. Virgin Classics (Veritas) 5620622.

CONCERTO GROSSO OP. 6, NO. 1 IN D MAJOR, Arcangelo Corelli
From *Corelli Concertos Opus 6*, Vol. 1, Philharmonia Baroque Orchestra; Nicholas McGegan, conducting. Harmonia Mundi Classical Express HCX 3957014.

TOCCATA IN D MINOR FOR ORGAN, BWV 913, J. S. Bach
From *Johann Sebastian Bach: Organ Works*; Gustav Leonhardt on the historical organ of Grote of St. Laurenskerk, Alkmaar, the Netherlands, built by Hagerbeer and Schnitger 1638–1725.

CHACONNE FROM DARDANUS, Jean-Philippe Rameau
From *Rameau: Suites from Platée & Dardanus*; Philharmonia Baroque Orchestra; Nicholas McGegan, conducting. Conifer Classics 75605 51313 2.

—VG

Program Music:
Overtures, Tone Poems, and Other Pieces that Appeal to the Senses

"Program music" is music that is based on a nonmusical source or whose structure is influenced by nonmusical material. Basically, it is music that tells a story or paints a picture. The golden age of program music was the 19th century, when Romantic artists rebelled against the abstract formality they felt constrained the art of the previous generation. Their ideal was to appeal to the heart and the senses, rather than to the intellect. Many pieces of program music are one-movement works, often called "overtures" or "tone poems" that try to capture the atmosphere of an exotic location or the plot of a literary work. Late 19th-century and 20th-century composers created longer works by stringing together individual movements united by a common theme. Prime examples are the six tone poems in Smetana's *Mà Vlast* ("*My Homeland*"), each of which describes a scenic feature or historical event from his native Bohemia, and the seven movements in Holst's *The Planets,* each devoted to a different heavenly body.

THE HEBRIDES OVERTURE, OP. 26, FINGAL'S CAVE, Felix Mendelssohn
From *Mendelssohn: Overtures,* London Symphony Orchestra, Claudio Abbado conducting, Deutsche Grammophon 2GH 423104

LES PRÉLUDES, Franz Liszt
From *Liszt: Symphonic Poems,* Polish Radio/TV Symphony Orchestra of Warsaw, Michael Halasz conducting, Naxos 8550487

VLTAVA (THE MOLDAU) FROM MÁ VLAST (MY HOMELAND),
Bedřich Smetana
From *Smetana: Má Vlast,* Boston Symphony Orchestra, Rafael Kubelik conducting, Deutsche Grammophon (DG Galleria) 2GGA 42918

TRAGIC OVERTURE, OP. 81, Johannes Brahms
From *The Klemperer Legacy - Brahms: Symphony no 1, &c.,* The Philharmonia Orchestra, Otto Klemperer conducting, EMI Classics CDM 7243 5 67029 2 9

NIGHT ON BARE MOUNTAIN, Modest Mussorgsky
From *Pictures at an Exhibition, &c.,* Ukrainian National Symphony Orchestra, Theodore Kuchar conducting, Naxos 8555924

TILL EULENSPIEGELS LUSTIGE STREICHE (TILL EULENSPIEGEL'S MERRY PRANKS), OP. 28, Richard Strauss
From *Strauss: Also sprach Zarathustra, &c.,* Vienna Philharmonic Orchestra, Herbert von Karajan conducting, London (Decca Legends) 2DM 466388

PRÉLUDE À L'APRÈS-MIDI D'UNE FAUNE, Claude Debussy
From *Debussy: La Mer, Nocturnes, Jeux, &c.,* Montreal Symphony Orchestra, Charles Dutoit conducting, London (Double Decca) 2LH2 460217

TAPIOLA, OP. 112, Jean Sibelius
From *Sibelius: Karelia Suite, Tapiola, &c.,* London Symphony Orchestra, Sir Colin Davis conducting, RCA 68770

RAPSODIE ESPAGNOLE, Maurice Ravel
From *Ravel: Bolero, Rapsodie Espagnole, &c.,* Boston Symphony Orchestra, Charles Munch con ducting, RCA Victor Gold Seal 6522

THE PLANETS, OP. 32, Gustav Holst
From *Gustav Holst: The Planets,* Philharmonia Orchestra, John Eliot Gardiner conducting Deutsche Grammophon 445 860-2

—VG

Symphonies

The modern symphony, as a musical form, evolved from the opera overture during the middle of the 18th century. Structured along the same
lines as the solo sonata and the string quartet, a symphony is a work for
orchestra, in several movements of differing character. Originally thought
of as providing lightweight entertainment, the symphony was trans-
formed by the great composers of the Classical era (Haydn, Mozart, and
Beethoven) into a vehicle for a composer's most profound thoughts.
Symphonies are usually abstract works that adhere to formal rules of
musical logic rather than obeying specifically dramatic or picturesque
inspiration, but in the 19th century many composers felt free to blur that
distinction. Symphonies began to follow literary models, or to evoke
scenery, or even to include voices, all the while remaining faithful to the
technical integrity of the form. In the later 20th century, the symphony
fell somewhat into neglect, as composers favored forms that allowed
greater freedom, but insightful artists such as John Adams have found
ways to inject life into the old tradition.

SYMPHONY NO. 40 IN G MINOR, K. 550, Wolfgang Amadeus Mozart
From *Mozart: Symphonies Nos. 40 & 41 "Jupiter,"* Vienna philharmonic
orchestra Orchestra; Leonard Bernstein, conducting. Deutsche
Grammophon Gesellschaft 445 548-2.

**SYMPHONY NO. 94 IN G MAJOR, SURPRISE (MIT DEM
PAUKENSCHLAG),** Franz Josef Haydn
From *Haydn: "London," "Surprise" & "Military" Symphonies,* Philharmonia
Hungarica; Antal Dorati, conducting. Decca (Penguin Classics)
2894606282.

SYMPHONY 5 IN C MINOR, OP. 67, Ludwig van Beethoven
From *Beethoven: Symphonien Nos. 5 & 7,* Vienna philharmonic orchestra;
Carlos Kleiber, conducting. Deutsche Grammophon Gesellschaft 447 400-2.

SYMPHONIE FANTASTIQUE, OP. 14, Hector Berlioz
From *Berlioz: Symphonie fantastique,* Orchestre Révolutionnaire et
Romantique; Sir John Eliot Gardiner, conducting. Philips 2894344022.

SYMPHONY NO. 8 IN B MINOR, D. 759, UNFINISHED, Franz Schubert
From */Mendelssohn: Symphony No.4/Schubert: Symphony No.8,*
Philharmonia Orchestra; Giuseppe Sinopoli, conducting. Deutsche
Grammophon Gesellschaft (Masters) 45514.

SYMPHONY NO. 4 IN A MAJOR, OP. 90, ITALIAN, Felix Mendelssohn
From *Mendelssohn: Symphonies No. 4 "Italian" (including Version of
1833/34) & No. 5 "Reformation,"* Vienna philharmonic orchestra; John
Eliot Gardiner, conducting. Deutsche Grammophon Gesellschaft 459 156-2.

SYMPHONY NO. 2 IN D MAJOR, OP. 73, Johannes Brahms
From *Brahms: Symphonies Nos. 2 & 3,* Oslo Philharmonic Orchestra.
Mariss Jansons, conducting. Simax PSC 1204.

SYMPHONY NO. 9 IN E MINOR, FROM THE NEW WORLD, Antonin Dvořák
From *Dvořák: Symphonies Nos. 8 & 9,* Berlin Philharmonic Orchestra;
Rafael Kubelik, conducting. Deutsche Grammophon 2GOR 447412.

SYMPHONY NO. 4 IN F MINOR, OP. 36, Peter Ilyich Tchaikovsky
From *Tchaikovsky: Symphony No. 4 and Romeo & Juliet,* London
Symphony Orchestra; George Szell, conducting. Decca (Penguin
Classics) 2DP 460655.

SYMPHONY NO. 2 IN D MAJOR, Jean Sibelius
From *Sibelius: Symphonies Nos. 2 & 7,* Philadelphia Orchestra; Eugene
Ormandy, conducting. Sony Classical (Essential Classics) SBK 53509.

SYMPHONY NO. 4 IN G MAJOR, Gustav Mahler
From *Mahler: Symphony No. 4,* San Francisco Symphony Orchestra with
Laura Claycomb; Michael Tilson Thomas, conducting. Delos SFS 0004.

SYMPHONY NO. 1 IN D MAJOR, OP. 25, CLASSICAL, Sergei Prokofiev
From *Prokofiev: Symphonies Nos. 1 & 4,* Scottish National Orchestra;
Neeme Järvi, conducting. Chandos Records CHAN 8400.

HARMONIELEHRE, John Adams
From *John Adams: Harmonielehre, etc.,* City of Birmingham Symphony
Orchestra; Simon Rattle, conducting. EMI Classics 7243 5 55051 2 5.

—VG

How the Brill Building
Saved Rock and Roll

Between Elvis Presley and the British Invasion, collections of assembly-line songwriters kept rock and roll going. Many of these teams worked out of and around the Brill Building in New York. Although they usually wrote under factory-like pressure, they crafted the warmest and much of the best popular music between the late 1950s and the middle of the 1960s.

BE MY BABY, the Ronettes (Jeff Barry and Ellie Greenwich with Phil Spector)
DA DOO RON RON, the Crystals (Barry and Greenwich with Phil Spector)
FOOLS FALL IN LOVE, the Drifters (Jerry Leiber and Mike Stoller)
HOUND DOG, Big Mama Thornton (Leiber and Stoller)
JAILHOUSE ROCK, Elvis Presley (Leiber and Stoller)
LEADER OF THE PACK, the Shangri-Las (Barry and Greenwich with Shadow Morton)
THE LOCO-MOTION, Little Eva (Gerry Goffin and Carole King)
ONE FINE DAY, the Chiffons (Goffin and King)
RIVER DEEP, MOUNTAIN HIGH, Ike and Tina Turner (Barry and Greenwich with Phil Spector)
STAND BY ME, Ben E. King (Leiber and Stoller)
UP ON THE ROOF, the Drifters (Goffin and King)
UPTOWN, the Crystals (Barry Mann and Cynthia Weil)
WE GOTTA GET OUT OF THIS PLACE, the Animals (Mann and Weil)
WILL YOU LOVE ME TOMORROW? the Shirelles (Goffin and King)
YAKETY YAK, the Coasters (Leiber and Stoller)
(YOU MAKE ME FEEL LIKE) A NATURAL WOMAN, Aretha Franklin (Goffin and King)
YOU'VE LOST THAT LOVIN' FEELIN', Righteous Brothers (Mann and Weil, with Phil Spector)

—CC

Blame It on
John Mayall

John Mayall is the godfather of the British blues. His legendary band, the Bluesbreakers, spawned the cream of 1960s-era British rock groups (including Cream itself). Mayall, now in his 70s, still plays and sounds great, but he will perhaps be best remembered for the superstars who got their start with the Bluesbreakers. Among them were Eric Clapton, Jack Bruce, Steve Winwood, Aynsley Dunbar, Mick Fleetwood, John McVie, and Mick Taylor. The Bluesbreakers' influence can be seen throughout an extraordinary extended family that includes Cream, Fleetwood Mac, Traffic, the Yardbirds, Led Zeppelin, the Rolling Stones, the Jeff Beck Group, and beyond.

BACK IN THE HIGH LIFE, Steve Winwood
BELL BOTTOM BLUES, Derek and the Dominoes
BORN UNDER A BAD SIGN, Cream
CAN'T FIND MY WAY HOME, Blind Faith
CROSSROADS, Cream
FEELIN' ALRIGHT, Traffic
FOR YOUR LOVE, the Yardbirds
HAD TO CRY TODAY, Blind Faith
HEART FULL OF SOUL, the Yardbirds
HIDEAWAY, John Mayall & the Bluesbreakers
JOHN BARLEYCORN MUST DIE, Traffic
LAYLA, Derek and the Dominoes
LOW SPARK OF HIGH-HEELED BOYS, Traffic
ONLY YOU KNOW AND I KNOW, Dave Mason
PEARLY QUEEN, Traffic
POLITICIAN, Jack Bruce
RIDIN' ON THE L & N, John Mayall & the Bluesbreakers
SPOONFUL, Jack Bruce
STRANGE BREW, Cream
SUNSHINE OF YOUR LOVE, Cream
TEARS IN HEAVEN, Eric Clapton

—MB

Jazz:
Struttin' the Mainline

Through the 1930s and 1940s, jazz in the form of the Big Band was the popular music of the day, filling dance halls and entertaining audiences around the country. However a new voice began to emerge toward the end of the war—frenetic, chaotic, and infused with emotional intensity. Charlie Parker, Dizzy Gillespie, Thelonius Monk, Charles Mingus, and others challenged the old ways and established a new and vital message. Another voice emerged from this group of musicians, one that continually shaped the style and form of the music for the remainder of the century—Miles Davis.

BLOOMDIDO, Charlie Parker and Dizzy Gillespie, *Bird and Diz*
BLUE RONDO À LA TURK, the Dave Brubeck Quartet, *Time Out*
THE SIDEWINDER, Lee Morgan, *The Sidewinder*
JACQUI, Clifford Brown and Max Roach, *Study in Brown*
FEE-FI-FO-FUM, Wayne Shorter, *Speak No Evil*
BLUE IN GREEN, Miles Davis, *Kind of Blue*
IN A SENTIMENTAL MOOD, Duke Ellington and John Coltrane, *Duke Ellington & John Coltrane*
YOU DON'T KNOW WHAT LOVE IS, Sonny Rollins, *Saxophone Colossus*
IT AIN'T NECESSARILY SO, Miles Davis, *Porgy and Bess*
DOLPHIN DANCE, Herbie Hancock, *Maiden Voyage*
IN WALKED BUD, Art Blakey's Jazz Messengers with Thelonious Monk, *Art Blakey's Jazz Messengers with Thelonious Monk*
'ROUND MIDNIGHT, Gerry Mulligan and Thelonious Monk, *Mulligan Meets Monk*
WEST COAST BLUES, Wes Montgomery, *The Incredible Jazz Guitar*
COUSIN MARY, John Coltrane, *Giant Steps*
BETTER GIT IT IN YOUR SOUL, Charles Mingus, *Mingus Ah Um*

—MHansen

Ah Um:
Charles Mingus

Charles Mingus was many things—an accomplished bassist and pianist, a published author, a label owner, a rumored schizophrenic—but mainly he was one of the most gifted jazz composers of all time. From the 1950s until he was diagnosed with Lou Gehrig's disease in the 1970s, Mingus pushed the boundaries of the jazz form, mixing big-band swing with bebop skronk, gospel euphoria, Dixieland strut, Latin percussion, and avant-garde otherworldliness. His compositions were just as wild, angry, heartfelt, and complex as he was.

EAST COASTING
EAT THAT CHICKEN
FABLES OF FAUBUS
GOODBYE PORK PIE HAT
GROUP DANCE
HAITIAN FIGHT SONG
HOG CALLIN' BLUES
MY JELLY ROLL SOUL
OH LORD, DON'T LET THEM DROP THAT ATOMIC BOMB ON ME
OPEN LETTER TO DUKE
PASSIONS OF A MAN
PEGGY'S BLUE SKYLIGHT
PITHECANTHROPUS ERECTUS
REINCARNATION OF A LOVEBIRD
SLOP
THE SHOES OF THE FISHERMAN'S WIFE ARE SOME JIVEASS SLIPPERS
TIJUANA GIFT SHOP
WEDNESDAY NIGHT PRAYER MEETING
WHAM BAM THANK YOU MA'AM

—DS

Jazz:
The Fusion Transfusion

Perhaps no other period of jazz spawned more controversy than that which became known as fusion. Reflecting the social tensions of the late 1960s and early 1970s, musicians sculpted new forms of music using the influences of rock, soul, and R & B as well as the expansive new technologies that were becoming available. Abandoning older methods, some artists sought to expand new boundaries in structure and rhythm, resulting in a new freedom of expression. Others used the same tools to achieve a lyrical, swinging beauty.

DONNA LEE, Jaco Pastorius, *Jaco Pastorius*
MILES RUNS THE VOODOO DOWN, Miles Davis, *Bitches Brew*
VITAL TRANSFORMATION, Mahavishnu Orchestra,
The Inner Mounting Flame
WATERMELON MAN, Herbie Hancock, *Head Hunter*
A REMARK YOU MADE, Weather Report, *Heavy Weather*
BRIGHT SIZE LIFE, Pat Metheny, *Bright Size Life*
SPAIN, Chick Corea, *Light as a Feather*
COBRA, Miles Davis, *Amandla*
WILLOW, Pat Martino, *Head & Heart*
BINKY'S BEAM, John McLaughlin, *Extrapolation*

—MHansen

Jazz:
Young Lions, Old Tigers, and Other Cool Cats

Building on the diversity of musical styles and forms from around the world as well as its own rich heritage, jazz continues to evolve. Reflecting the richness of our shared experiences, the music can be colorful, conflicted, and inspiring—revealing jazz to be a living and expressive art.

PIOGGIA DI PERUGIA, Jeremy Pelt, *Close to My Heart*
FOREST FLOWER: SUNRISE/SUNSET, Charles Lloyd, *Voices in the Night*
FOR ALL YOU ARE, Dave Holland, *Not for Nothing*
WINTER, Patricia Barber, *Modern Cool*
WHEN I FALL IN LOVE, Keith Jarrett, Gary Peacock, Jack DeJohnette, *Inside Out*
SINCE YOU ASKED, John Scofield, *Time on My Hands*
PEEL ME A GRAPE, Diana Krall, *Love Scenes*
ANYTHING GOES, Brad Mehldau, *Anything Goes*
CINCO QUATRO, Tom Harrell, *The Art of Rhythm*
SHELBY STEELE WOULD BE MOWING YOUR LAWN, Don Byron, *Music for Six Musicians*
HARD GROOVE, Roy Hargrove Presents the RH Factor, *Hard Groove*
VARIATIONS (ON A CONSPIRACY THEORY), Russell Gunn, *Ethnomusicology Volume 3*
CREPUSCULE WITH NELLIE, T. S. Monk, *Monk on Monk*
NEVER BROKEN (ESP), Cassandra Wilson, *Traveling Miles*
BODY AND SOUL, Joe Lovano, *From the Soul*

—MHansen

Bluegrass Junction:
Songs for Getting High and Lonesome

In the hills of Kentucky, Bill Monroe invented a whole new genre. And American music was never the same again.

ANGEL BAND, the Stanley Brothers
DOOLEY, the Dillards
BLUE MOON OF KENTUCKY, Bill Monroe
FOGGY MOUNTAIN BREAKDOWN, Flatt & Scruggs
ROLL IN MY SWEET BABY'S ARMS, Del McCoury
LAST TRAIN, Peter Rowan
LONG BLACK VEIL, Country Gentlemen
BABY, NOW THAT I'VE FOUND YOU, Alison Krauss
ARKANSAS TRAVELER, Norman Blake
THE YEE-HAW FACTOR, Béla Fleck
GREAT SPECKLED BIRD, Jim & Jesse
ROCKY TOP, the Osborne Brothers

—DM

The Stanley Brothers:
Songs for Weepin', Dancin', and Prayin'

Bill Monroe is rightfully called the father of bluegrass, but nobody exemplifies the "high, lonesome sound" quite like Ralph and Carter Stanley. Ralph Stanley's plaintive, otherworldly tenor harmonies are forever stamped on the history of American music.

RANK STRANGERS

MAN OF CONSTANT SORROW

MIDNIGHT RAMBLE

LITTLE MAGGIE

ORANGE BLOSSOM SPECIAL

SHE'S MORE TO BE PITIED

GATHERING FLOWERS FOR THE MASTER'S BOUQUET

PRETTY POLLY

TRAIN 45

HARD TIMES

DRINKING FROM THE FOUNTAIN

LITTLE MAGGIE

CLINCH MOUNTAIN BACKSTEP

HOW MOUNTAIN GIRLS CAN LOVE

THINK OF WHAT YOU'VE DONE

—DM

American Roots:
Songs for Discovering Where It All Began

Some people say there really is no true American music. We respectfully disagree, and we offer these songs as proof.

A BIG BALL IN COWTOWN (WE'LL DANCE AROUND),
Bob Wills & His Texas Playboys
JOHN HARDY, Carter Family
SUGAR BABY, Dock Boggs
MATCH BOX BLUES, Blind Lemon Jefferson
ROLL DOWN THE LINE, Uncle Dave Macon
THE RIVER OF JORDAN, the Louvin Brothers
LOVESICK BLUES, Hank Williams
I'M MOVING ON, Hank Snow
TRAIN WHISTLE BLUES, Jimmie Rodgers
STUCK UP BLUES, Roy Acuff
IF YOU'VE GOT THE MONEY (I'VE GOT THE TIME), Lefty Frizzell
WALKIN' THE FLOOR OVER YOU, Ernest Tubb

—DM

Songs for Enjoying
Country Music Without Embarrassment

Shucks, most a-them fellers on the radio are all hat, no cattle. "Alternative country" is where you can still find the real deal.

ABSOLUTELY SWEET MARIE, Jason and the Scorchers
FACTORY BELT, Uncle Tupelo
ST. IGNATIUS, Old 97's
BLACK SOUL CHOIR, 16 Horsepower
EXCUSE ME WHILE I BREAK MY OWN HEART TONIGHT, Whiskeytown
SEE HIM ON THE STREET, the Jayhawks
RIGHT IN TIME, Lucinda Williams
SIN CITY, Flying Burrito Brothers
I PUSH RIGHT OVER, Robbie Fulks
HONKY TONK MAN, Dwight Yoakam
WAITRESS SONG, Freakwater
GUITAR TOWN, Steve Earle

—DM

Positively Bob Dylan

The center couldn't hold for long, of course, but in 1965 Bob Dylan had cornered the world's supply of cool. Striking sparks from the collision of folk and rock and roll, Dylan founded a style, a spiel, and a sound that forged a new cutting edge in popular music. Look: At the height of his own popularity, *John Lennon* wanted to be this guy! While Dylan has drifted in and out of listenability in the decades since, any alt-rocker unaware of his early, blistering electric oeuvre should check into the nearest reeducation camp *now* for immediate regrooving.

HIGHWAY 51 BLUES
ONLY A PAWN IN THEIR GAME
MOTORPSYCHO NIGHTMARE
SUBTERRANEAN HOMESICK BLUES
LIKE A ROLLING STONE
HIGHWAY 61 REVISITED
STUCK INSIDE OF MOBILE WITH THE MEMPHIS BLUES AGAIN
LEOPARD-SKIN PILL-BOX HAT
ALL ALONG THE WATCHTOWER
TANGLED UP IN BLUE

—MR

The 1960s "Folk Scare"

The roots of modern American folk music run straight through Woody Guthrie and the Great Depression. In the '60s, a new generation of singers took up the cause and for a moment broke into the mainstream of American music—scaring older generations of folk artists as well as some of the general public.

ALICE'S RESTAURANT, Arlo Guthrie
GIVE YOURSELF TO LOVE, Kate Wolf
GOLDEN APPLES OF THE SUN, Judy Collins
HALLELUJAH, Leonard Cohen
HOW LONG, Odetta
MARY HAMILTON, Joan Baez
RAMBLING BOY, Tom Paxton
SAILING DOWN MY GOLDEN RIVER, Pete Seeger
ST. JAMES INFIRMARY, Dave Van Ronk
TALKING DUST BOWL BLUES, Woody Guthrie
THE HOUSE I LIVE IN, Josh White
THE JOY OF LIVING, Ewan MacColl
THE MARY ELLEN CARTER, Stan Rogers
THE URGE FOR GOING, Joni Mitchell
WASN'T THAT A TIME, the Weavers

—SH

The Continuing
Folk Tradition

Following the '60s, a new group of artists made folk music their own and continued to drive the style.

BARBED WIRE BOYS, Susan Werner
FOLLOW THAT ROAD, Anne Hills
GANDHI/BUDDHA, Cheryl Wheeler
GOOD NOISE, John Gorka
LUCILLE, Fred Eaglesmith
METAL DRUMS, Patty Larkin
RICH MAN'S WAR, Steve Earle
RIVERSIDE, Eliza Gilkyson
TANGLEWOOD TREE, Dave Carter and Tracy Grammer
THE BABYSITTER'S HERE, Dar Williams
THESE COLD FINGERS, Bill Morrissey
TIDE AND THE RIVER RISING, Cindy Kallet
TRANSIT, Richard Shindell
WHEN THE FIRST LEAVES FALL, Steve Gillette and Cindy Mangsen
WHO WOULDA THUNK IT, Greg Brown

—SH

The Folk Youngsters

Folk isn't dead, folks. A new generation of singers is gaining a foothold in the music business and continuing to extend the folk heritage.

A BEND IN THE RIVER, Mark Erelli
BAD SHOES BLUES, the Mammals
CARDS ON THE TABLE, Lisa Moscatiello
EIGHTH LIT WINDOW, Rachael Davis
FIGARO, Jerree Small
4 & 20 BLUES, Jeffrey Foucault
OCEAN OR A TEARDROP, David Jacobs-Strain
OH DEATH, Rani Arbo and Daisy Mayhem
PLOW TO THE END OF THE ROW, Adrienne Young and Little Sadie
SOUL OF A MAN, Ollabelle
THE LEAVING, Jeff Black
TWO KIDS, Anais Mitchell

—SH

Folk-Rock-Country
Kaleidoscope

There are certain communities of musicians who, over the course of many years, form groups, split up, regroup, split up again to work solo, and regroup again for reunion concerts (and to play tributes to departed members). Each recombination produces something distinctive yet familiar. One of the richest sources of these recombining gems in the North American country-folk-rock scene, starting in the 1960s and continuing today, centered on Gram Parsons, Stephen Stills, Roger McGuinn, David Crosby, Graham Nash, Neil Young, Richie Furay, Chris Hillman, J. D. Souther, and others. Pick your mood—electric or acoustic, political or sentimental—these guys combine some of the best songwriting, the best harmony, and the best guitar around.

BLUEBIRD, Buffalo Springfield
BUS STOP, the Hollies
CARRY ON/QUESTIONS, Crosby, Stills, Nash, & Young
DARK END OF THE STREET, Gram Parsons
DIM LIGHTS, THICK SMOKE (AND LOUD, LOUD MUSIC), the Flying Burrito Brothers
EIGHT MILES HIGH, the Byrds
FOR WHAT IT'S WORTH, Buffalo Springfield
49 BYE-BYES, Crosby, Stills, & Nash
HELPLESSLY HOPING, Crosby, Stills, & Nash
HICKORY WIND, Gram Parsons
IF I NEEDED SOMEONE, the Hollies
IF YOU GOTTA GO, GO NOW, the Flying Burrito Brothers
I'LL FEEL A WHOLE LOT BETTER, the Byrds
LOVE THE ONE YOU'RE WITH, Crosby, Stills, Nash, & Young
MR. SOUL, Buffalo Springfield
MY BACK PAGES, the Byrds
SATISFIED MIND, the Flying Burrito Brothers
SO BEGINS THE TASK, Manassas
SUITE: JUDY BLUE EYES, Crosby, Stills, & Nash
TURN, TURN, TURN, the Byrds

—MB

Early Joni Mitchell

If you hear the name Joni Mitchell and think "Both Sides Now" or "The Circle Game," then give a listen to this playlist. Her early work has intelligent poetry, innovative arrangements, and (before the decades of chain-smoking) a clear soprano voice. She set the pace for generations of introspective songwriters to come, and yet these songs still sound fresh.

A CASE OF YOU
BANQUET
BLUE
CALIFORNIA
CAREY
COLD BLUE STEEL AND SWEET FIRE
COURT AND SPARK
DOWN TO YOU
JUDGEMENT OF THE MOON AND STARS (LUDWIG'S TUNE)
JUST LIKE THIS TRAIN
LESSON IN SURVIVAL
MY OLD MAN
RIVER
WILLY
YOU TURN ME ON I'M A RADIO
CACTUS TREE

—KRyer

Folk Protest

It's not like you want to live in a period that needs protest songs, but a good collection is timeless.

BLOWIN' IN THE WIND, Bob Dylan
EVE OF DESTRUCTION, Barry Maguire
I-FEEL-LIKE-I'M-FIXIN'-TO-DIE RAG, Country Joe & the Fish
FORTUNATE SON, Creedence Clearwater Revival
FROM WAY UP HERE, Pete Seeger
I AIN'T MARCHIN' ANYMORE, Phil Ochs
MASTERS OF WAR, Bob Dylan
NO MAN'S LAND, Eric Bogle
OHIO, Crosby, Stills, Nash, & Young
SKY PILOT, Eric Burdon & the Animals
SO LONG, MOM; I'M OFF TO DROP THE BOMB, Tom Lehrer
THE BAND PLAYED WALTZING MATILDA, the Pogues
UNIVERSAL SOLDIER, Donovan
WAR, Edwin Starr
WHERE HAVE ALL THE FLOWERS GONE, Pete Seeger

—LK/MHamilton/MR

Punk Protest

These are not your father's protest songs—because this is not your father's protest.

%&*@ AUTHORITY, Pennywise
FRANCO UN-AMERICAN, NOFX
WALK THE WALK, Face to Face
STAND YOUR GROUND, Rancid
WEIGH ON MY MIND, Transplants
ALL RISE, Jersey
LAND OF THE FREE? Pennywise
WAVE THE FLAGS, Happy Campers
CAN'T WE ALL JUST GET ALONG, Guttermouth
PRISONER OF SOCIETY, Living End
OPERATION RESCUE, Bad Religion
COME JOIN US, Bad Religion
RAISE YOUR VOICE, Bad Religion

—RB

The Building Blocks
of Punk

The seeds of Punk were planted ten years before the music pushed up in Manhattan, London, and dozens of other cities.

RUN RUN RUN, Velvet Underground
KICK OUT THE JAMS, the MC5
NO FUN, the Stooges
SHE CRACKED, the Modern Lovers
TRASH, the New York Dolls
FINAL SOLUTION, Rocket from the Tombs
SEE NO EVIL, Television
BLANK GENERATION, Richard Hell & the Voidoids
I JUST WANNA HAVE SOMETHING TO DO, Ramones
SONIC REDUCER, Dead Boys
ASK THE ANGELS, Patti Smith
CHINESE ROCKS, Johnny Thunders & the Heartbreakers
ANARCHY IN THE U.K., the Sex Pistols
SAFE EUROPEAN HOME, the Clash
PULLED UP, Talking Heads
RIP HER TO SHREDS, Blondie
ANOTHER GIRL ANOTHER PLANET, the Only Ones

—BW/MR

Jonathan Richman

"I created Jonathan [Richman]," punk godfather Lou Reed is reputed to have said, "but I won't be held responsible for him." Indeed, Richman has blazed his own trail since his early days as a Velvet Underground acolyte. The first electric incarnation of his protean band, the Modern Lovers, set the tone for generations of straight-edge punk geeks; subsequent iterations pushed the acoustic envelope with its exploration of childlike themes and stripped-down sounds. In recent years, Richman has reclaimed the legacy of his formative years while bringing it into line with the antiheroics of his current stage persona.

ROADRUNNER
MODERN WORLD
I'M STRAIGHT
DODGE VEG-O-MATIC
HEY THERE LITTLE INSECT
ABDUL AND CLEOPATRA
BACK IN YOUR LIFE
VINCENT VAN GOGH
GIVE PARIS ONE MORE CHANCE
I WAS DANCING IN THE LESBIAN BAR
VELVET UNDERGROUND

—MR

Required Ramones:
Gabba Gabba Hey!

It's just not fair, but an enduring rock-and-roll legacy doesn't ensure personal longevity. Consider the cruel fate of the Ramones, three of whom have died within the past four years. Vocalist Joey Ramone went first, in 2001. Bassist and main songwriter Dee Dee passed a year later, and guitarist Johnny succumbed in September 2004. Tommy, the drummer who left the lineup early in the band's grueling 20-year career, is now the lone surviving founder. Formed in 1974, the Ramones poked a pinhead into '70s pop excess, playing perfect pop songs at express-train speeds.

BLITZKREIG BOP
PINHEAD
I WANNA BE SEDATED
JUDY IS A PUNK
SUZY IS A HEADBANGER
SHEENA IS A PUNK ROCKER
TOO TOUGH TO DIE
ROCK & ROLL HIGH SCHOOL
TEENAGE LOBOTOMY
GIMME GIMME SHOCK TREATMENT
PSYCHO THERAPY
WE'RE A HAPPY FAMILY
BEAT ON THE BRAT
I WANNA BE YOUR BOYFRIEND
I WANT YOU AROUND
COMMANDO
ROCKAWAY BEACH
CRETIN HOP
NOW I WANNA SNIFF SOME GLUE
NEEDLES AND PINS
ANXIETY
MY BRAIN IS HANGING UPSIDE DOWN (BONZO GOES TO BITBURG)
R.A.M.O.N.E.S.
WHAT A WONDERFUL WORLD, Joey Ramone

—MF

Barrettes, Vintage Dresses, and Guitars: Riot Grrl Anthems

Riot Grrls represented both a social movement and the musical phenomenon of angry women who rocked.

CHERRY BOMB, the Runaways
50 FOOT QUEENIE, PJ Harvey
I'M IN THE BAND, Bratmobile
I'M NOT WAITING, Sleater-Kinney
I'M NOT YOUR MOTHER, Blake Babies
LADYKILLERS, Lush
OH BONDAGE, UP YOURS, X-Ray Spex
NO ONE'S LITTLE GIRL, the Raincoats
REBEL GIRL, Bikini Kill
WHERE THE GIRLS ARE, the Gossip

—MF

Quiet Is the New Loud:
Belle & Sebastian

Belle & Sebastian is this generation's J. D. Salinger, Smiths, and John Hughes all rolled into one. Since 1996, the Scottish band has been marrying delicate vocals and orchestral, folk-inspired arrangements to heartfelt lyrics that explore fragile lives. Impossibly pretty and heartbreakingly rendered, the group's songs weave together the religious and the profane, the spiteful and the melancholy, the stark and the sweet.

A CENTURY OF FAKERS
DIRTY DREAM NUMBER TWO
DOGS ON WHEELS
GET ME AWAY FROM HERE, I'M DYING
I DON'T LOVE ANYONE
I KNOW WHERE THE SUMMER GOES
IF SHE WANTS ME
IF YOU'RE FEELING SINISTER
I'M A CUCKOO
JUDY AND THE DREAM OF HORSES
LE PASTIE DE LA BOURGEOISIE
LIKE DYLAN IN THE MOVIES
MY WANDERING DAYS ARE OVER
PHOTO JENNY
PUT THE BOOK BACK ON THE SHELF
SEEING OTHER PEOPLE
SHE'S LOSING IT
STARS OF TRACK AND FIELD
STRING BEAN JEAN
THE BOY WITH THE ARAB STRAP
THE ROLLERCOASTER RIDE
THE STATE I AM IN
THERE'S TOO MUCH LOVE
WE RULE THE SCHOOL
WRAPPED UP IN BOOKS

Bonus List!

Over time, Belle & Sebastian have inspired a slew of artists from around the world; we've included a few of their like-minded peers from the British Isles.

EMMA'S HOUSE, Field Mice
FALLING FROM GRACE, the Gentle Waves
HAIR LIKE ALAIN DELON, White Town
(I WANT YOU) MORE THAN EVER, the Clientele
NOTHING LEFT TO SAY, Tram
ONLY LOVE CAN BREAK YOUR HEART, Saint Etienne
SOMETIMES I STILL FEEL THE BRUISE, Trembling Blue Stars
SONG FOR BABY, Isobel Campbell
STRIKE ME DOWN, Reindeer Section
SUSPENDED FROM CLASS, Camera Obscura
THESE THINGS, Looper

—DS

Slanted and
Enchanted: '90s Indie Rock

Even with Nirvana and a slew of other alternative-rock bands making the big time in the 1990s, plenty of talented acts still went unrecognized. These indie-rock groups recorded for small labels, played in small clubs, and sold small numbers of CDs. Occasionally they built up a large enough following to get signed by the major labels, but usually they spent time—in the words of the Liquor Giants' Ward Dotson—"rewriting history while the whole world's ignoring me."

CALIFORNIA, Quasi
CAR, Built to Spill
DEAREST DARLING, Liquor Giants
DEFINITION OF LOVE, Don Lennon
DOIN' THE COCKROACH, Modest Mouse
$%&@ AND RUN, Liz Phair
GOLDFISH BOWL, Smog
HOLLAND 1945, Neutral Milk Hotel
JUMPING FENCES, the Olivia Tremor Control
LICENSE TO CONFUSE, Sebadoh
LONG DIVISION, the Aislers Set
MY MY METROCARD, Le Tigre
PSYCHOSOMATICA, Bedhead
SLACK @!#%, Superchunk
SUGARCUBE, Yo La Tengo
SUMMER BABE, Pavement
TELL ME NOW, Boy, Scrawl
TIDAL WAVE, Apples in Stereo
TRACTOR RAPE CHAIN, Guided by Voices
WAITING FOR THE KID TO COME OUT, Spoon
MY FORGOTTEN FAVORITE, Velocity Girl

—DS

Air Guitar

OK. So here is the weird thing: Whenever we told someone we were working on this book, more often than not, the person would ask, "Are you doing an air guitar playlist?" Well, yes, we are.

GODZILLA, Blue Oyster Cult
ERUPTION/YOU REALLY GOT ME, Van Halen
TOM SAWYER, Rush
BACK IN BLACK, AC/DC
SMOKE ON THE WATER, Deep Purple
SUNSHINE OF YOUR LOVE, Cream
WHOLE LOTTA LOVE, Led Zeppelin
WE WILL ROCK YOU, Queen
WILD THING, the Troggs
THE BOYS ARE BACK IN TOWN, Thin Lizzy
SHE SELLS SANCTUARY, the Cult
SHOULD I STAY OR SHOULD I GO, the Clash
GIMME ALL YOUR LOVIN', ZZ Top
FOR WHOM THE BELL TOLLS, Metallica
PARANOID, Black Sabbath
SULTANS OF SWING, Dire Straits
20TH CENTURY BOY, T. Rex
ACE OF SPADES, Motorhead
STILL OF THE NIGHT, Whitesnake
RUN TO THE HILLS, Iron Maiden

—AP

Mandatory Metallica

A collection of songs from the band that yelled the loudest about illegal downloads.

HARVESTER OF SORROW
DISPOSABLE HEROES
FIGHT FIRE WITH FIRE
THE FOUR HORSEMEN
EYE OF THE BEHOLDER
WELCOME HOME
TO LIVE IS TO DIE
METAL MILITIA
LEPER MESSIAH
NOTHING ELSE MATTERS
ENTER SANDMAN
CREEPING DEATH
FOR WHOM THE BELL TOLLS
SEEK AND DESTROY
FADE TO BLACK
THE UNFORGIVEN
THE UNFORGIVEN II
PHANTOM LORD
HIT THE LIGHTS
MASTER OF PUPPETS
NO LEAF CLOVER
JUMP IN THE FIRE
DIE, DIE MY DARLING
ST. ANGER
MOTORBREATH

—RB

The Damage Done:
Songs for Admitting That You Have a Problem

Got a monkey on your back? Perhaps the two of you can enjoy these songs together. Think of it as the 13th step.

WHISKEY BOTTLE, Uncle Tupelo
COCAINE BLUES, Rev. Gary Davis
HEROIN, Velvet Underground
DEAD FLOWERS, Townes Van Zandt
THERE STANDS THE GLASS, Webb Pierce
OVER THE HILL, Ten Years After
SISTER MORPHINE, the Rolling Stones
CCKMP, Steve Earle
SAM STONE, John Prine
MOONSHINER, Cat Power
SAD BUT TRUE, Metallica
THE NEEDLE AND THE DAMAGE DONE, Neil Young
COLD TURKEY, John Lennon
BLED WHITE, Elliot Smith
THE DRUNKARD'S DOOM, Louvin Brothers
SOBER, Tool

—DM

Songs in the Key
of Death: Music for Meeting Your Maker

We all have to die and pay taxes. But for some reason, there are only a few songs about paying taxes.

THE END, the Doors
O DEATH, Ralph Stanley
IN MY TIME OF DYIN', Bob Dylan
TWO WHITE HORSES, Blind Lemon Jefferson
THE ART OF DYING, George Harrison
STRANGE FRUIT, Billie Holiday
GLOOMY SUNDAY, Lydia Lunch
SEE THAT MY GRAVE IS KEPT CLEAN, Lightnin' Hopkins
I JUST WANNA DIE, Geto Boys
AND WHEN I DIE, Blood, Sweat & Tears
DEATH IS NOT THE END, Nick Cave and the Bad Seeds
LET THE TRAIN BLOW THE WHISTLE, Johnny Cash
KNOCKIN' ON HEAVEN'S DOOR, Warren Zevon

—DM

Jazz Funeral

The New Orleans tradition of funerals with music stretches back hundreds of years. A brass band plays music for the funeral procession: On the way to the cemetery, the songs are somber and mournful; on the way back home, the band picks it up.

AS I LAY MY BURDEN DOWN, Magnificent Seventh's Brass Band
BURGUNDY STREET BLUES, George Lewis
DIDN'T HE RAMBLE, Preservation Hall Jazz Band
DOWN BY THE RIVERSIDE, George Lewis
FEEL SO GOOD, Magnificent Seventh's Brass Band
IN THE SWEET BY AND BY, Preservation Hall Jazz Band
JUST A CLOSER WALK WITH THEE, Eureka Brass Band
LEAD ME SAVIOR, Magnificent Seventh's Brass Band
OLD RUGGED CROSS, Preservation Hall Jazz Band
WALK THROUGH THE STREETS OF THE CITY,
Preservation Hall Jazz Band
WHAT A FRIEND WE HAVE IN JESUS, Preservation Hall Jazz Band
WHEN THE SAINTS GO MARCHING IN, George Lewis

—CB

Beyond Monster Mash:
Songs for a Halloween Party

It's not enough to throw a couple bags of fun-sized candy bars in a bowl when Halloween rolls around. For kids of most ages, this is *the* holiday of the year. So live it up a little. Put on a vampire's cape. Dress up as a buccaneer. Heck, just slap on an eye patch. And put on some spooky songs for this All Hallow's Eve. Oh, and one more tip: Don't give out raisin boxes. Kids hate those.

BAD MOON RISING, Creedence Clearwater Revival

BATMAN, Danny Elfman

BELA LUGOSI'S DEAD, Bauhaus

CEMETERY GATES, the Smiths

CREATURE FROM THE BLACK LAGOON, Dave Edmunds

CREEP, Radiohead

DEAD MAN'S PARTY, Oingo Boingo

DEAD SOULS, Joy Division

DEVIL DOLL, X

DEVIL'S HAIRCUT, Beck

DIRTY CREATURE, Split Enz

DRAGULA, Rob Zombie

EATEN BY THE MONSTER OF LOVE, Sparks

(EVERYDAY IS) HALLOWEEN, Ministry

FRANKENSTEIN, Aimee Mann

FRANKENSTEIN, Edgar Winter Group

(GHOST) RIDERS IN THE SKY, Johnny Cash

GHOST TOWN, the Specials

GHOSTBUSTERS, Ray Parker Jr.

HALLOWEEN (SHE GETS SO MEAN), Rob Zombie

I PUT A SPELL ON YOU, Screamin' Jay Hawkins

I WALKED WITH A ZOMBIE, Roky Erickson and the Aliens

I WAS A TEENAGE WEREWOLF, the Cramps

IT'S HALLOWEEN, the Shaggs

KILLING MOON, Echo and the Bunnymen

LIVING DEAD GIRL, Rob Zombie

MONSTER IN MY PANTS, Fred Schneider

MONSTER MASH, Bobby Boris Pickett and the Crypt-Kickers
PEOPLE ARE STRANGE, the Doors
PET CEMETERY, Ramones
PSYCHO KILLER, Talking Heads
RING OF FIRE, Wall of Voodoo
SCARY MONSTERS (AND SUPER CREEPS), David Bowie
SEASON OF THE WITCH, Donovan
SPELLBOUND, Siouxsie and the Banshees
SPOOKY, Classics IV
STRANGE, REM
STRANGE BREW, Cream
SUPER FREAK, Rick James
SUPERSTITION, Stevie Wonder
TALES FROM THE CRYPT, Danny Elfman
THE GHOST IN YOU, the Psychedelic Furs
THE MUNSTERS THEME, Comateens
THE PURPLE PEOPLE EATER, Sheb Wooley
THE TIME WARP, the Rocky Horror Picture Show
THRILLER, Michael Jackson
TUBULAR BELLS, Mike Oldfield
TWILIGHT ZONE, Golden Earring
WELCOME TO MY NIGHTMARE, Alice Cooper
WEREWOLVES OF LONDON, Warren Zevon
WITCHCRAFT, Frank Sinatra
ZOMBIE, the Cranberries

—RB/CC

A Rockin' Good Holiday: Rock and Roll Holiday Songs

Rock and roll has always done a good job of embracing the holidays. You won't find a better rock-and-roll Christmas album than *A Christmas Gift for You from Phil Spector,* but many singers still give their all for the seasons.

2000 MILES, the Pretenders
A CHANGE AT CHRISTMAS (SAY IT ISN'T SO), the Flaming Lips
ALL I WANT FOR CHRISTMAS IS YOU, Carla Thomas
BACK DOOR SANTA, Clarence Carter
BLUE CHRISTMAS, Elvis Presley
CHRISTMAS (BABY, PLEASE COME HOME), Darlene Love, U2
CHRISTMAS SONG, Dave Matthews Band
THE CHRISTMAS SONG, Weezer
CHRISTMAS WRAPPING, the Waitresses
CHRISTMASTIME, Smashing Pumpkins
DECK THE HALLS, Red Hot Chili Peppers
DO THEY KNOW IT'S CHRISTMAS? Band Aid
FATHER CHRISTMAS, the Kinks
FEELS LIKE CHRISTMAS, Al Green
HAPPY XMAS (WAR IS OVER), John Lennon
HAVE YOURSELF A MERRY LITTLE CHRISTMAS, the Pretenders
I SAW MOMMY KISSING SANTA CLAUS, the Jackson 5
I WANT AN ALIEN FOR CHRISTMAS, Fountains of Wayne
I WON'T BE HOME FOR CHRISTMAS, Blink-182
JINGLE BELL ROCK, the Moonglows
JINGLE BELLS, Brian Setzer Orchestra
LET'S MAKE CHRISTMAS MEAN SOMETHING THIS YEAR, James Brown
LITTLE DRUMMER BOY, Joan Jett
LITTLE DRUMMER BOY/PEACE ON EARTH, Bing Crosby and David Bowie
LITTLE SAINT NICK, the Beach Boys
LONELY CHRISTMAS EVE, Ben Folds

MERRY CHRISTMAS BABY, Charles Brown, Otis Redding
MERRY CHRISTMAS (I DON'T WANT TO FIGHT TONIGHT), Ramones
PLEASE COME HOME FOR CHRISTMAS, Charles Brown
ROCKIN' AROUND THE CHRISTMAS TREE, Brenda Lee
RUN RUDOLPH RUN, Chuck Berry
SANTA CLAUS, They Might Be Giants
SANTA CLAUS IS COMING TO TOWN, the Crystals, Bruce Springsteen
SILENT NIGHT, Cyndi Lauper
SLEIGH RIDE, the Ronettes
SONG FOR A WINTER'S NIGHT, Sarah McLachlan
SOUL CHRISTMAS, Graham Parker
STEP INTO CHRISTMAS, Elton John
THANKS FOR CHRISTMAS, XTC
THE CHANUKAH SONG, Adam Sandler
WHITE CHRISTMAS, Clyde McPhatter & the Drifters
WINTER WONDERLAND, Darelene Love, Eurythmics

—CC

Chestnuts Roasting:
Traditional Holiday Songs

It's always wise to have a good, swinging collection of traditional songs around for when the relatives come by. You don't want to alienate your mother-in-law by putting on "Grandma Got Run Over by a Reindeer," do you? Put on your Santa hat, pour yourself a hefty mug of eggnog, and let the wholesomeness seep in.

A SONG FOR CHRISTMAS, Natalie Cole
AULD LANG SYNE, Guy Lombardo
BABY, IT'S COLD OUTSIDE, Louis Armstrong
CAROL OF THE BELLS, Wynton Marsalis
CAROLING, CAROLING, Manhattan Transfer
CHRIST IS BORN, Perry Como
CHRISTMAS IS COMING, Vince Guaraldi Trio
CHRISTMAS MEDLEY, Liberace
CHRISTMAS TIME IS HERE, Vince Guaraldi Trio
DECK THE HALLS, Nat King Cole
DO YOU HEAR WHAT I HEAR? Anne Murray
FELIZ NAVIDAD, Jose Feliciano
THE FIRST NOEL, Ella Fitzgerald
FROSTY THE SNOWMAN, Gene Autry, Jimmy Durante
GREENSLEEVES, John Coltrane
HARK! THE HERALD ANGELS SING, Mitch Miller and the Gang
HAVE A HOLLY JOLLY CHRISTMAS, Burl Ives
HAVE YOURSELF A MERRY LITTLE CHRISTMAS,
Frank Sinatra, the Carpenters
HERE COMES SANTA CLAUS, Gene Autry
HOW THE GRINCH STOLE CHRISTMAS, Boris Karloff
I HEARD THE BELLS ON CHRISTMAS DAY, Harry Belafonte
I SAW MOMMY KISSING SANTA CLAUS, Jimmy Boyd
I'D LIKE YOU FOR CHRISTMAS, Julie London
I'LL BE HOME FOR CHRISTMAS, Harry Connick Jr.
IT CAME UPON A MIDNIGHT CLEAR, Julie Andrews
IT MUST HAVE BEEN THE MISTLETOE, Barbra Streisand
IT'S BEGINNING TO LOOK A LOT LIKE CHRISTMAS, Johnny Mathis

IT'S THE MOST WONDERFUL TIME OF THE YEAR, Rosemary Clooney
JINGLE BELL ROCK, Bobby Helms
JINGLE BELLS, Etta James, Les Paul
JOLLY OLD SAINT NICHOLAS, Eddy Arnold
JOY TO THE WORLD, Nat King Cole
LET IT SNOW! LET IT SNOW! LET IT SNOW! Dean Martin
LINUS AND LUCY, Vince Guaraldi Trio
MY FAVORITE THINGS, Tony Bennett
O COME ALL YE FAITHFUL, Bing Crosby
O HOLY NIGHT, Johnny Mathis
OLE SANTA, Dinah Washington
PRETTY PAPER, Roy Orbison
ROCKIN' AROUND THE CHRISTMAS TREE, Brenda Lee
RUDOLPH THE RED-NOSED REINDEER, Burl Ives
SANTA BABY, Eartha Kitt
SANTA CLAUS IS COMING TO TOWN, Patti Page
SILENT NIGHT, Perry Como, Dinah Washington
SILVER AND GOLD, Burl Ives
SILVER BELLS, Mike Douglas
SKATING, Vince Guaraldi Trio
SLEIGH RIDE, Ella Fitzgerald
THE CHIPMUNK SONG (CHRISTMAS DON'T BE LATE), the Chipmunks
THE CHRISTMAS SONG, Vince Guaraldi Trio
THE CHRISTMAS SONG (CHESTNUTS ROASTING), Nat King Cole
THE CHRISTMAS WALTZ, Doris Day
THE LITTLE DRUMMER BOY, the Harry Simeone Chorale
WELCOME CHRISTMAS, Boris Karloff
WHAT ARE YOU DOING CHRISTMAS EVE? Nancy Wilson
WHAT CHILD IS THIS? Mel Torme
WHITE CHRISTMAS, Bing Crosby
WINTER WONDERLAND, Ray Charles
ZAT YOU, SANTA CLAUS? Louis Armstrong

—CC

Index

You've Had a Look, Now Take a Listen!

Reading about the perfect iMix playlists is fun, but actually listening to them is even better, which is why we've made links to the iMixes featured in this book available at the Peachpit Web site. Just click on a link to buy the entire playlist from Apple's iTunes Music store. Head to **www.peachpit.com/playlistbook** and rock out to your favorite iMixes today!

While you're shopping for playlists at the Peachpit site, we invite you to post your comments about each iMix and let us know which songs we left out, which ones should have never made the cut, and why you just can't get enough of **Nina Simone**, **Eminem**, **Ashlee Simpson**, **Johnny Cash**, **The White Stripes**, **The Clash**, or whomever else rocks your world. Blog on today. We want to hear from you!

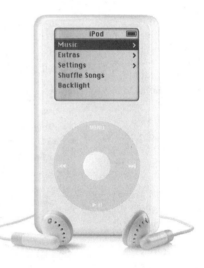